The Alchemy of Affection

The Alchemy of Affection:

Unveiling the Mysteries of Lasting Love

Dr. Kevin Grold

Author of

The Love Report

The Alchemy of Affection

Copyright © 2023 Kevin M. Grold Ph.D.

All rights reserved.

ISBN: 978-1-0881-4164-9

INTRODUCTION

Welcome to *The Alchemy of Affection*, your step-by-step manual for love. You will discover the essential elements necessary for creating a meaningful connection and the secrets to unlocking a profound and enduring love. Practical tips, relatable examples, and transformative exercises will help you integrate this complex subject to make it as clear and accessible as possible.

Much like an alchemist who carefully blends and refines their ingredients to create a precious substance, you too will have the tools to cultivate a beautiful and fulfilling relationship through knowledge, dedication, and desire. *The Alchemy of Affection* will guide you as you navigate the challenges and opportunities that arise on your path to lasting love.

Join me on this adventure as we unravel the mysteries of love together. Be inspired, empowered, and ignited by the flame of passion within you, guiding you toward a love story that transcends time.

Turn the pages, open your heart, and be guided to the love you deserve.

THE STEP-BY-STEP MANUAL FOR LOVE

DEDICATION

After losing his wife Christine to breast cancer, Dr. Grold is honoring her memory by donating all profits from his book to help cancer patients obtain wigs. Losing hair during cancer treatment can be a traumatic experience, and having access to wigs can help ease the emotional burden. Unfortunately, many individuals cannot afford this crucial part of the healing process. Dr. Grold's donation aims to fill this gap and provide much-needed support to those struggling to feel normal during a difficult time.
www.ebeauty.com (4/4 stars on CharityNavigator.org)

Thank you for purchasing *The Alchemy of Affection*. I hope you find value in reading it. Please consider leaving a review online. Your feedback allows me to reach more people and help others who need wigs while dealing with cancer. Please go to https://tinyurl.com/AlchemyRev if you would like to leave a review.

Dr. Kevin Grold

CONTENTS

INTRODUCTION 4

DEDICATION 5

Part I

The Ingredients of Love

CHAPTER 1: UNDERSTANDING ATTRACTION: AN IMPORTANT KEY TO LOVE 10

CHAPTER 2: COMMITMENT: THE BEDROCK OF LOVE 32

CHAPTER 3: EFFECTIVE COMMUNICATION: THE JUICE 51

CHAPTER 4: TRUST: THE FOUNDATION FOR LASTING LOVE 71

Part II

The Alchemy of Healing and Transformation

CHAPTER 5: REMOVING BARRIERS TO LOVE 96

CHAPTER 6: CONFLICT: TURNING CHALLENGES INTO GROWTH 118

CHAPTER 7: FORGIVENESS: HEALING WOUNDS TO STRENGTHEN YOUR BOND 137

CHAPTER 8: COMPASSION: CULTIVATING EMPATHY WITH YOUR SOULMATE 153

Part III

The Gold of Love

CHAPTER 9: MINDFULNESS: THE ART OF LOVING ATTENTION 166

CHAPTER 10: GRATITUDE: CULTIVATING APPRECIATION 178

CHAPTER 11: SERVICE: EXPRESSING LOVE THROUGH ACTION 191

Part IV

The Everlasting Bond of Love

CHAPTER 12: PASSION: CULTIVATING A SEXUAL BOND 202

CHAPTER 13: MAINTAINING INTIMACY IN A LOVING RELATIONSHIP 227

CHAPTER 14: TRANSCENDENT LOVE: FINDING THE DIVINE IN YOUR PARTNERSHIP 242

CONCLUSION: THE ALCHEMICAL JOURNEY OF LOVE 252

HOPE FOR LOVE 259

ABOUT THE AUTHOR 261

How to be successful using *The Alchemy for Affection*:

- Acknowledge that you and your partner may have different levels of enthusiasm for improving your relationship.
- Don't pressure your partner to learn from this book if they're not ready.
- Ask if they would like to set aside time to read it together.
- Start with one section of the book you think you both would find interesting.
- Make the experience positive and rewarding for your partner.
- Once they've had a positive experience, they'll likely want to continue.

With patience, positivity, open-mindedness, forgiveness, and commitment, you can use this manual to create a stronger, more loving relationship.

Dr. Kevin Grold

Part I: The Ingredients of Love

CHAPTER 1: UNDERSTANDING ATTRACTION: AN IMPORTANT KEY TO LOVE

This chapter delves into the biology and psychology of attraction, exploring what draws people to each other in order to unlock an essential key to understanding love. It covers the science of pheromones, the role of dopamine and oxytocin in bonding, and the importance of similarity and reciprocity in relationship formation. It also examines some common pitfalls and misconceptions about attraction, such as the idea that opposites attract or that physical attractiveness is the essential factor. Readers can better understand the crucial difference between love and attraction by first understanding the science of **attraction.**

The Science and Biology of Attraction

Our bodies are designed to seek out and connect with potential partners. The biological aspects of attraction are powerful and fascinating, from releasing hormones like dopamine and oxytocin to activating specific brain regions.

When attracted to a potential mate, our brains release a cocktail of chemicals that create a pleasurable feeling. Dopamine, a neurotransmitter associated with pleasure and reward, floods the brain when we experience something we enjoy. This can include everything from good food to engaging in sexual activity.

PRO TIP

Pay attention to your body's signals. Notice how you feel when you are around someone you are attracted to and be mindful of the sensations in your body. This understanding can help you tune into your desires and make better mindful decisions about who you pursue.

*** *** ***

Research shows that physical touch, even something as simple as holding hands or hugging, can increase feelings of attraction and connection.

Example

Lila and Alex met at a party and hit it off immediately. Lila noticed that when they were talking, her heart rate increased, and she felt a fluttering sensation in her stomach. She decided to trust her instincts and ask Alex out. They held hands and hugged during their date, which deepened their connection and set the foundation for their attraction.

Another hormone associated with attraction is oxytocin, also known as the "cuddle hormone." Oxytocin is released during physical touch, including hugging, holding hands, and sexual activity. This hormone is associated with feelings of bonding and trust, making it crucial in developing an attraction to your partner.

The Role of Pheromones

Pheromones are chemical signals or scents emitted by our bodies and detected by others. While the exact role of pheromones in human attraction is still being studied, research suggests that they play a role in mate selection. Numerous studies, such as by the National Institutes of Health, have shown that women may be more attracted to men whose scent indicates a strong immune system, while men may be more attracted to women whose scent indicates fertility.

PRO TIP

Pay attention to the enticing aromas and sensory experiences that arise when you find yourself in the presence of someone who captivates you. Stay attuned to the physical responses within your body, fostering a heightened sense of awareness. By cultivating this mindfulness, you will gain greater control over your reactions and prevent your mind from slipping into autopilot mode.

The Psychology of Attraction

Attraction is more than physical; our psychological and emotional states also influence our desire. From our personal histories to our beliefs and values, our individual experiences also shape who we are attracted to and why.

The Power of Similarity

Similarity in values, interests, and personality traits is vital to relationship satisfaction and longevity. We are more likely to build a solid foundation for lasting love when we are attracted to someone who shares our core values and passions.

Example

Tessa and Jess met through mutual friends and quickly realized they shared a love of travel and adventure. They bonded over their shared experiences and interests and felt an instant connection. As they got to know each other better, they discovered they also had similar family, career, and spiritual values. This deepened their connection and enabled them to build a lasting, fulfilling relationship.

Attachment Styles

Attachment styles are deeply ingrained patterns of relating and forming emotional bonds with others. They stem from early childhood experiences and interactions with caregivers, shaping our beliefs, expectations, and behaviors in relationships throughout our lives. There are three main attachment styles: secure, anxious, and avoidant.

Secure attachment is considered the ideal attachment style, characterized by a healthy balance of independence and intimacy. Those with a secure attachment style feel secure in their relationships, have a favorable view of themselves and their partners, and are comfortable with both closeness and autonomy. They have a strong foundation of trust, effective communication, and emotional support. Securely attached individuals can navigate challenges and conflicts in relationships with confidence and resilience.

Anxious attachment is marked by a fear of abandonment and a strong need for reassurance and validation from their partners. Those with an anxious attachment style often have heightened sensitivity to cues of potential rejection or abandonment, leading to frequent worries and anxieties about the stability of their relationships. They tend to seek constant closeness and validation, fearing that their partners may not be fully available or committed. This attachment style may stem from inconsistent or unpredictable caregiving during childhood, leading to deep-seated relationship insecurity.

Avoidant attachment is characterized by a strong desire for independence and a tendency to avoid emotional closeness and intimacy. Individuals with an avoidant attachment style may value self-reliance and self-sufficiency above all else, often maintaining emotional distance in relationships to protect themselves from potential hurt or vulnerability. They may struggle with expressing or acknowledging their own emotions and may find it challenging to provide emotional support to their partners. This attachment style can result from caregivers who were emotionally distant or unavailable during childhood, leading to learned self-reliance and a fear of dependency.

It's important to note that attachment styles are not fixed or set in stone. They can evolve and change over time, influenced by new experiences, personal growth, and therapeutic interventions. Developing a secure attachment style is possible through self-awareness, emotional healing, and cultivating healthy relationship dynamics. Understanding attachment styles can help individuals gain insights into their own patterns of relating and foster more fulfilling and secure connections with their partners.

It is essential to understand your attachment style as well as the attachment style of your partner. This can help you navigate potential conflicts and build a stronger, more fulfilling relationship. *For more details on this topic, take a look at the book Attachment* by Amir Levine and Rachel Heller.

Example

Saria and David had been dating for several months when Saria noticed that she was starting to feel anxious whenever David did not respond to her messages right away. She realized that she had an anxious attachment style, causing her to worry unnecessarily. She decided to talk to David about her concerns and was relieved that he was understanding and supportive. Together, they worked on building trust and open communication, which helped to alleviate Saria's anxieties.

PRO TIP

Communicate openly and honestly about your attachment style and any concerns or fears you may have. Be mindful of any patterns in your past relationships and how they may influence your current attachment style. Consider seeking therapy if you need support addressing past traumas or relationship patterns. These suggestions can increase the likelihood of building a robust and lasting connection.

The Social Factors of Attraction

Our social environments also influence who we are attracted to and why. Our social networks can influence our dating preferences and behaviors from cultural norms, peer pressure, and societal expectations. Our experiences and upbringing shape our understanding of love and relationships, and it is essential to be aware of these influences on your experience of attraction and love.

PRO TIP

Be mindful of external influences. Consider how your friends, family, and community may shape your views. Are there certain expectations or pressures you feel you need to conform to? By being aware of these influences, you can make more thoughtful choices about who you pursue, which will help guide your emotional response.

Culture and Attraction

Cultural norms and expectations play a significant role in how we approach relationships. For example, in some cultures, arranged marriages are still common, while dating and courtship are the norm in others. Understanding the cultural context of attraction can help us better understand our preferences and relationship approach.

Gender Roles and Expectations

Gender roles and expectations also play a role in attraction and relationships. For example, that men should be the breadwinners and women should be the caregivers. These expectations can create conflict and strain in relationships; it is essential to be aware of them.

Reflect on your cultural background, gender roles, and societal pressures and how they may influence your attraction toward others. Consider seeking partners who share your cultural values and experiences and be ready for the issues any differences may engender.

Familiarity

While exposure to novelty can increase attraction and connection, familiarity can also play a role in fostering attraction. Familiarity can increase liking and attraction in romantic relationships.

One reason for this is the "Mere-Exposure Effect", a psychological phenomenon where people tend to develop a preference for things they are repeatedly exposed to. In the context of relationships, the more time we spend with someone, the more likely we are to develop feelings of attraction toward them. This is because familiarity breeds a sense of comfort and security, which can create a deeper emotional connection with the other person.

In addition, familiarity can also facilitate emotional bonding by enabling us to understand and appreciate our partner's unique qualities and quirks. As we become more familiar with someone, we develop a deeper understanding of their thoughts, feelings, and behaviors, which can foster empathy and intimacy.

Example

Juanita grew up in a conservative household where traditional gender roles were strongly emphasized. When she started dating Maria, who was more progressive in her views, Juanita struggled to reconcile her beliefs with her partner's. After a series of honest and open conversations, Juanita realized that she needed to challenge her assumptions and be more open to different perspectives. She and Maria built a robust and fulfilling bond based on mutual respect and understanding.

PRO TIP

Based on what you have learned in this chapter, identify and deeply understand what causes you to feel attracted to a partner and consider how that may influence your relationship decisions.

Here Are Some More Ideas to Help You Cultivate Healthy Attraction

Exercise

List your core values and interests and use them as a guide when choosing partners or evaluating your current union. Are you and your partner aligned in these areas? Are there areas where you could deepen your connection by exploring shared interests or values?

Example

Maria and Juan both love outdoor activities like hiking and camping. They make it a priority to plan regular outdoor adventures together, which not only deepens their connection but also helps them stay physically active and mentally refreshed.

Childhood Unmet Needs

Our experiences and childhood influences shape our needs and desires in our current relationships. To have a fulfilling partnership, it is important to identify and understand these deep needs and work on understanding them when we are trying to meet them with our partner.

We often are attracted to partners who reflect our primary caregivers' positive and negative qualities. When we enter into a partnership, our unresolved childhood wounds can manifest in the form of a childish desire, when unmet, can lead to conflict or dissatisfaction with our partner. Understanding and addressing these deep needs creates a deeper connection with our partner.

For example, let's say that one partner had a parent who was emotionally unavailable during their childhood. This may have resulted in a deep need for emotional intimacy and validation in their adult relationships. If their partner does not meet this need, it may lead to very strong feelings of rejection or neglect.

Couples can work together to create a more intimate and validating bond by identifying and communicating this overly accentuated need to their partner. Overall, it is important to understand and address our deep needs in our relationships. Doing so can create more fulfilling and satisfying unions that meet our emotional and psychological needs.

PRO TIP

To delve into and better understand this important topic, read Harville Hendrix's excellent book, *Getting the Love You Want*.

***   ***   ****

One exercise for couples to better understand how their deep unmet childhood issues influence their current union, is "the childhood timeline." This exercise involves creating a timeline of significant events and experiences from each partner's childhood that may influence their current relationship.

Childhood Timeline Exercise

Caution: Do not do this exercise without professional help if you feel it could trigger memories of past trauma.

Step 1: Set aside dedicated time and comfortable space for sharing childhood stories.

Step 2: Each partner creates a timeline of significant events and experiences from their childhood, starting from their earliest memories and going up until their teenage years. This timeline will include both positive and negative experiences, as well as any significant relationships or traumas.

Step 3: Once the timelines are complete, partners take turns sharing their timelines. The sharing partner explains each significant event or experience in detail, focusing on how it impacted them emotionally and how it may be influencing their current relationship.

Step 4: The other partner actively listens and asks questions to clarify and better understand their partner's experiences and emotions. They also try to identify any patterns or themes that may be emerging, such as recurring feelings of abandonment or mistrust.

Step 5: After both partners have shared their childhood timelines, they can discuss emerging patterns or themes and explore how they may influence their current relationship. This may also involve discussing any unmet needs or unresolved wounds from their childhood and exploring how they may impact their interactions with their partner.

By identifying and addressing these deep unmet needs and unresolved wounds, couples can work toward creating a deeper and more fulfilling union based on mutual understanding and empathy.

IMPORTANT LEARNING FROM THIS CHAPTER:
All the above suggestions, tips, and exercises have been designed to help you understand and improve your attraction. **Be aware that we have NOT been discussing love; we have been discussing attraction.** You must CLEARLY understand the influence of attraction in order to experience the difference between attraction and love.

Dr. Kevin Grold

Change your Words, Change your Thinking, Change your Life Technology™

Do you use "I love" to describe your feelings toward ice cream, the weather, or even someone you just met? If you reserve the words "I love you" for someone you have a committed and communicative relationship with, you may avoid confusion when those casual dates don't work out. It's crucial to be clear and specific about words such as "love." By understanding what we truly mean by love and the other words we use to describe our emotions, we can better align our desires and experiences and cultivate a deeper sense of love in our lives.

Conclusion

It is critical to understand the difference between attraction and love. Research suggests that attraction is a complex interplay of biological, psychological, and social factors. We have discussed the role of hormones such as dopamine and oxytocin, the impact of attachment styles on relationships, and how cultural norms and gender roles shape our understanding of love and relationships. By recognizing the influence of attraction, you are one step closer to understanding and nourishing love in your life.

♥♥

CHAPTER 2: COMMITMENT THE BEDROCK OF LOVE

Have you ever wondered why some couples stay together for decades while others break up after just a few months? When two people commit to each other, they agree to cultivate their love and prioritize their relationship over the long term.

Commitment is a promise to stay together and a mindset that requires effort, dedication, and sacrifice. It means sometimes putting your partner's needs before your own and working through the inevitable challenges in any relationship. When deeply committed, you will put in the time and effort necessary to make your relationship work.

A commitment between two loving people is built on mutual trust, respect, and shared values. Several vital aspects are essential for creating a solid and lasting commitment in a relationship:

Honesty: Honesty is a crucial aspect of any commitment. It means being truthful with your partner about your thoughts, feelings, and actions, even when uncomfortable. Honesty creates a sense of transparency and trust in the relationship and helps to foster a deeper emotional connection between partners.

Working on the Relationship: A commitment requires ongoing effort and investment. Both partners must be willing to work to maintain and strengthen the relationship over time.

This can include regular communication, sharing experiences, and prioritizing the relationship.

Fidelity: Fidelity is a fundamental aspect of many committed relationships. It means being faithful to your partner, both emotionally and physically, and honoring the boundaries and agreements that have been established within the relationship.

Open Communication: Clear communication is vital in a committed relationship — Partners need to be willing to communicate openly and honestly with each other, even when it's complicated. This means actively listening to each other, expressing needs and concerns, and working together to solve any issues.

Mutual Respect: Respect is essential in any committed relationship. It means valuing your partner's feelings, thoughts, and needs. Mutual respect also means accepting each other's differences and working to understand and appreciate them.

Emotional Support: A strong commitment involves being there for your partner in both good times and bad. It means providing emotional support and encouragement and offering a listening ear or a shoulder to cry on when needed.

Shared Goals and Values: Partners truly committed to each other most often share similar goals and values. This can mean working together toward common goals, such as building a family or achieving financial stability. It can also mean sharing similar values around religion, politics, or social issues.

Acceptance and Forgiveness: No relationship is perfect. Partners committed to each other will inevitably experience challenges and conflicts. Acceptance and forgiveness are crucial aspects of a strong commitment. This means accepting one another's flaws and forgiving each other when mistakes are made.

Quality Time: Spending quality time together is essential to a firm commitment. This can mean engaging in activities both partners enjoy, such as traveling, trying new hobbies, or simply relaxing and enjoying each other's company.

Mutual Growth and Support: Partners committed to each other support each other's growth and development. This can mean encouraging each other to pursue personal or professional goals and providing support and guidance.

Flexibility and Adaptability: Life is unpredictable, and partners committed to each other must be flexible. This means adjusting to changing circumstances and challenges and being open to new opportunities and experiences.

*** *** ***

By prioritizing honesty, working on the relationship, fidelity, open communication, mutual respect, emotional support, shared goals, and values, acceptance and forgiveness, quality time, mutual growth and support, and flexibility, partners can create a deep and lasting bond that can withstand the test of time. *Yes, that is a long list. The idea is not to be perfect but instead to work on the areas of commitment that are most important to you and your partner.*

PRO TIP

Be sure you have communicated with your partner about what commitment means to your relationship. First, understand commitment clearly in your mind and then make sure you and your partner are on the same page. This is the most common mistake couples make: thinking that one's partner understands commitment the same way they do, without discussing it.

*** *** ***

The benefits of commitment are numerous. When you commit

to your partner, you create a sense of security in your relationship. You can find solace in the unwavering dedication and support of your partner. They demonstrate a steadfast commitment to standing by your side through all the ups and downs, providing assurance that they are there for you no matter what. This sense of security enables you to be vulnerable and open with your partner, leading to deeper intimacy and connection.

Commitment also fosters trust and respect in a relationship. When you commit to your person, it strengthens your bond. In essence you are saying, "I value you and our relationship enough to prioritize *us*."

Harper and Sarah

Harper and Sarah had been together for two years when they hit a rough patch. Harper had been working long hours, and Sarah felt she needed more attention from him. They were arguing more often and felt like they were growing apart.

The Alchemy of Affection

Instead of giving up on their relationship, Harper and Sarah decided to recommit to each other. They sat down and had a heart-to-heart about their feelings and concerns and exactly what each meant by their commitment to the other. They planned to set aside time each week to spend together, whether it was a date night or just a quiet evening at home. They also agreed to be more intentional about showing love and appreciation for each other. As a result of their discussions about commitment, Harper and Sarah's relationship improved dramatically. They felt closer and more connected and could quickly work through future challenges.

Exercise
1. Have a heart-to-heart with your partner about your commitment.
2. Discuss your feelings and concerns and decide to increase your commitment to each other.
3. Ensure you know what commitment means to you and express this to your partner.

IMPORTANT: MAKE SURE YOU ARE NOT MIND-READING WHAT YOUR PARTNER IS THINKING ABOUT WHAT COMMITMENT MEANS IN YOUR RELATIONSHIP.

Mark and Emily

Mark and Emily had been together for five years and were considering marriage, but they hesitated to make such a big commitment. They had seen friends and family members go through divorces and did not want to end up in the same situation. Instead of letting their fears hold them back, Mark and Emily approached their relationship with even more resolve. They took a premarital counseling course together, which helped them identify areas where they needed to grow as a couple. They also talked openly and honestly about their values and goals and planned their future together. As a result of their deepened commitment, Mark and Emily felt more confident in their relationship. They knew they were in it for the long term and were willing to work through any challenges that came their way. They married a year later and have been creating a positive relationship ever since.

Your commitment can include the following agreements:
To be honest;
To not have sex with others;
To not flirt with others;
Not to make supportive, solid emotional bonds with others of the opposite sex if you're straight, or same-sex if homosexual;

To work on the relationship;

To stay when times are tough.

To support each other

(add your own ideas)

*** *** ***

Written Agreement

Here's an example of what an agreement between two loving people might look like. The agreement below has many items so you can choose the ones important to you and your relationship.

Love Commitment Agreement Example Between Logan and Robin

Date: [insert date]

Logan and Robin declare our love for each other and our commitment to building and maintaining a relationship built on trust, mutual respect, and deep affection.

We agree to the following commitments:

The Alchemy of Affection

Honesty: We vow to be truthful with each other, to communicate openly, and create a safe and supportive space where we can share our thoughts, feelings, and ideas without fear of judgment or rejection.

Fidelity: We pledge our loyalty to each other, promising to remain faithful to our love, to cherish and honor each other, and to be each other's loyal companion and partner.

No flirting: We pledge to abstain from any behaviors seen as flirting with others, as we believe our love is a sacred bond to be always be protected and cherished.

Emotional bonds: We promise to avoid forming strong emotional bonds with others of the opposite sex (if heterosexual) or same sex (if homosexual) that could threaten our relationship.

Working on the relationship: We commit to investing time, energy, and effort into our relationship, as we believe it is worth it to create a loving and lasting bond.

Staying during tough times: We pledge to stay together and support each other through the ups and downs of life, as we believe our love is strong enough to overcome any obstacle that may come our way.

Supporting each other: We vow to help each other emotionally, physically, and mentally, to prioritize each other's well-being, and create a loving, nurturing environment where we can thrive and flourish.

Respect: We commit to treating each other with respect and compassion and never belittle, demean, or criticize each other.

Trust: We vow to trust each other fully and to be *trustworthy* in all our actions and decisions.

Forgiveness: We pledge to forgive each other for mistakes, misunderstandings, and shortcomings and to work toward reconciliation and healing.

Intimacy: We commit to cultivating intimacy in our physical and emotional relationship and to creating a safe and sacred space where we can express our love and affection freely and without reservation.

Growth: We vow to support each other's personal growth and development and to encourage each other to pursue our dreams and aspirations.

Gratitude: We commit to expressing gratitude and appreciation for each other regularly and to celebrate our relationship.

Flexibility: We pledge to adapt in our relationship and be open to change and growth as our love evolves.

Communication: We commit to communicating openly, honestly, and respectfully with each other and actively listening and responding to each other's needs and concerns.

Shared values: We vow to honor and respect each other's values, beliefs, and principles and to work toward creating a shared vision for our life together.

Quality time: We pledge to spend quality time together to create meaningful experiences and memories and to prioritize our relationship above other obligations and distractions.

The Alchemy of Affection

Shared responsibilities: We commit to sharing responsibilities and duties in our relationship and supporting each other in achieving a healthy work-life balance.

Personal space: We vow to respect each other's need for space and independence and to create a healthy balance between togetherness and separateness.

Laughter and joy: We pledge to bring joy, laughter, and playfulness into our relationship and cherish the moments of fun we share.

Passion: We commit to cultivating passion and excitement, to keep the flame of our love burning bright, and to pursue intimacy with enthusiasm and joy.

Romance: We vow to keep the romance alive in our relationship by surprising each other with thoughtful gestures and tokens of affection — be it a last-minute flight to Rome or cooking their favorite pasta.

Financial: We will not do things that will harm our financial stability and growth together. We vow to discuss large purchase items in advance.

Patience: We vow to practice patience and understanding in our relationship, be gentle and give each other time and space to grow and flourish.

Growth: We pledge to support each other's evolution, to be each other's anchors and guides, and encourage each other to become the best version of ourselves.

Adventure: We vow to embark on adventures together, explore new opportunities, and create a life filled with wonder, excitement, and joy.

We understand that building a solid and loving relationship is a lifelong journey. We are committed to embarking on this journey together, as we believe our love is worth it.

Signed,

[Logan's signature] [Robin's signature]

Ideas for Your Discussion Regarding Commitment

Commitment Ceremony: You can plan a ceremony to affirm your commitment publicly or privately. This can include exchanging vows, exchanging rings or other meaningful symbols, and possibly involving family and friends to witness and support your commitment.

Relationship Contract: You can create a formal contract outlining the terms of your commitment to each other. This can include communication, boundaries, fidelity, and financial responsibility agreements.

Consequences: The contract can also outline consequences for violations of the agreement and provide a framework for conflict resolution.

Personalized Rituals: You can create personalized rituals that help to reinforce your love and commitment to each other. This can include cooking meals together, going on regular date nights, or creating a shared gratitude practice.

Relationship Check-Ins: You can commit to regular relationship check-ins, where you reflect on your progress and discuss any issues or challenges. This can strengthen your communication skills and build trust and intimacy in your relationship.

Joint Goal Setting: You can set mutual goals that align with your shared vision for the future. This can include financial, career, or personal growth goals; or goals related to the relationship. They can strengthen your bond and create a shared purpose by working toward these goals together.

Acts of Service: You can commit to performing regular acts of service for each other. This can include cooking meals, doing laundry, running errands, and more emotional actions such as listening attentively or providing emotional support.

Physical Touch: You can prioritize physical touch as a way to reinforce your love and connection. This can include regular cuddling, holding hands, or engaging in sexual intimacy.

*** *** ***

Conclusion

Overall, there are many different ways that a couple can solidify their love and commitment to each other. The key is to discuss your commitment and what it means to both of you and for you to solidify it in whatever way you choose. Ultimately, the form that an agreement between two people takes will depend on your unique needs and desires. The key is to have open and honest communication and to take concerted steps to nurture and solidify your love for each other.

The most significant benefit of commitment is the longevity it can bring to a relationship. Committing to your partner makes you less likely to give up on the relationship when things get tough. Instead, you are willing to work through challenges and grow together as a couple. This can lead to a lifetime of love and happiness.

Commitment is a significant key to cultivating love that lasts a lifetime. By putting in the effort to prioritize your relationship and work through challenges together, you can create a deep sense of intimacy and connection with your partner.

Commitment is not just a promise; it is a mindset that can transform your relationship and bring you closer than ever.

CHAPTER 3: EFFECTIVE COMMUNICATION: THE JUICE

Communication is the cornerstone of any healthy relationship. The ability to express your thoughts and feelings, and to listen to and understand your partner, is essential for building a robust and lasting connection. In this chapter, we will provide practical tips for improving your communication, offer exercises to help you put these strategies into practice, and share examples of these tips used to build stronger relationships.

Couples deepen their relationship when they communicate

openly and honestly about their thoughts, feelings, and needs. This includes being willing to listen to each other without judgment and expressing empathy and understanding when one's partner shares something sensitive. Poor communication can lead to misunderstandings, hurt feelings, and even relationship breakdowns.

Effective communication enables partners to:

Express their thoughts and feelings: Communication enables partners to share their thoughts, feelings, and needs. This helps to build trust and emotional intimacy.

Resolve conflicts: Effective communication can help couples resolve disputes in a healthy and constructive manner. It enables both partners to listen to each other's perspectives and find a mutually agreeable solution.

Build deeper emotional connections: Communication is

essential for building a deep relationship with your partner. When you share details of not only your day but open your soul, you create a safe space for each other to be vulnerable and share your true selves.

Practical Tips for Improving Communication

Listen actively: Active listening means giving your partner your full attention when they are speaking. This means avoiding distractions such as your phone or the TV, maintaining eye contact, and providing verbal cues that you are engaged in the conversation.

Use "I" statements: When expressing your thoughts and feelings, use "I" statements rather than "you" statements. For example, say, "I feel hurt when you do/say that," instead of, "You always do/say that, and it makes me angry." The "I statement" approach is less accusatory and helps to avoid defensiveness in your partner.

Practice empathy: Empathy means understanding your partner's perspective and feelings. It involves putting yourself in their shoes. This can help to build compassion and understanding in your relationship.

Take breaks during conflicts: It is often essential to calm down and collect your thoughts before continuing a conversation. This can help prevent a situation from escalating, enabling both partners to approach the conflict with clear heads.

Practice active problem-solving: Active problem-solving requires working together. This involves identifying the problem, brainstorming solutions, and choosing the best course of action together.

Emotionally Honest Conversations: Another critical aspect of communication is learning to express your thoughts and feelings clearly and honestly. This can be challenging, especially when dealing with difficult emotions or navigating a thorny topic. However, it is crucial to communicate openly with your partner to build a solid foundation of trust and mutual understanding. Opening up slowly with difficult topics hopefully elicits an understanding response from your partner, and you can continue to be vulnerable with more difficult issues. Choose a topic that is important to you and one that you may have felt unsure about discussing. Set aside some agreed-upon time for an emotionally honest conversation. Be open about your concerns and encourage your partner to do the same. Remember to stay calm and respectful, *especially* if you disagree.

Couples Using Effective Communication to Improve Their Relationship

Martha and Riley

Martha and Riley had been married for five years and struggled with communication. They would often argue about trivial issues and have difficulty resolving conflicts. They decided to seek the help of a couples therapist who provided them with tools for improving communication. They started practicing active listening and empathy and used "I" statements to express themselves. They also took breaks during conflicts to calm down before continuing to talk. Over time their communication improved, and they could resolve disputes more effectively.

Exercises for Improving Communication

Practice Empathy

Empathy means putting yourself in your partner's shoes, acknowledging their feelings, and validating their experiences, even if you disagree.

1. Choose a topic you and your partner disagree on and reframe the situation from their perspective.
2. Imagine how they feel and why they might feel that way.
3. Share your insights.

To practice empathy, be sure to:

1. Reflect on what you hear to show that you understand.
2. Ask open-ended questions to better understand your partner's perspective. For example, don't ask "are you mad" or "are we ok?" Rather, ask "What are you feeling right now? What can I do to make it better?"
3. Avoid minimizing or dismissing your partner's feelings, even if you disagree.

Emily and Mark

Emily and Mark had been together for two years and were having trouble communicating about their needs in the relationship. They often assumed the other person knew what they wanted and became resentful when their needs were unmet. They started practicing active problem-solving and communicating more openly about their expectations. As a result, their relationship grew stronger, and they felt more connected.

Active Listening

One vital key to effective communication is learning to listen actively, fully concentrating on your partner's words without interrupting or preparing your response. When you actively listen, you show that you value your person's thoughts and feelings, which can help them feel more understood and appreciated.

Active listening involves fully engaging with your partner when they are speaking rather than just waiting for your turn to talk. You are paying attention to their words, body language, and tone of voice and demonstrating that you understand what they are saying.

Active Listening Practice

1. Set aside time with your significant other to practice active listening.
2. Take turns speaking and listening, and practice fully concentrating on your partner's words without interrupting or preparing your response.
3. After each exchange, summarize what you heard to ensure you understand your partner's message before continuing.
4. Make sure your partner agrees with your summary before you continue.

To practice active listening, be sure to:

1. Make eye contact with your partner.
2. Avoid interrupting them.
3. Use nonverbal cues, like nodding or smiling, to show engagement.
4. Wait until your partner is finished, and then repeat what they have said in your own words to ensure you both agree that you understand.
5. If your partner disagrees that you heard what was said, try again.

PRO TIP

DO NOT SOLVE THE PROBLEM. When practicing Active Listening, ask yourself, "Am I providing a solution to the problem presented?" If the answer is yes, then you are not actively listening correctly. It is important to remember that active listening does not require you to provide a solution and can be counterproductive. It can make the speaker feel like you are not listening and prevent them from fully opening up.

Mind Reading

Mind reading involves assuming you know your partner's thoughts or feelings without asking them. It can lead to misunderstandings, hurt feelings, and a communication breakdown.

Instead of Mind Reading, try the Following

Ask open-ended questions to gain a deeper understanding of your partner's perspective.

Avoid assuming you know what your person is thinking or feeling. Practice active listening to truly hear your partner's words and emotions.

Dr. Kevin Grold

Couples Using Effective Communication

Mark and Sarah

Mark and Sarah have been together for five years. Early on in their relationship, they would often argue, and both felt unheard and frustrated. One day, Mark suggested using "I" statements when expressing their feelings. They also started practicing active listening and empathy. Over time, they began feeling more connected and understood, and their fights became less frequent and intense.

Reflective Writing: Reflect on your worries about and hopes for your relationship. Jot your reflections in a journal or notebook, then share with your partner. This can help you communicate more effectively and deepen your emotional connection.

PRO TIP

If you are having trouble with communication, do not give up hope. It is common not to be good at a skill we were never taught. Consider a few sessions with a counselor if you get stuck. The lessons learned will be valuable and beneficial throughout your life.

Additional Exercises for Improving Communication

The Empathy Exercise

The Empathy Exercise involves practicing empathy by striving to understand your partner's perspective, even if you disagree. This exercise helps to build connection and trust in your relationship.

To do the Empathy Exercise:

1. Choose a topic to discuss

2. Practice listening to your partner's perspective without judgment or criticism.
3. Reflect on what you are hearing to show your understanding.

Practice validating your partner's emotions, even if you disagree with their perspective. Try your best to experience what they are feeling, perhaps by closing your eyes and meditating on it, to fully understand the feelings in your body.

The "I" Statements Exercise

The "I" Statements Exercise involves practicing expressing your thoughts and feelings using "I" statements instead of "you" statements. This helps you to take ownership of your emotions and avoid blaming or criticizing your partner.

To do the "I" Statements Exercise:

1. Choose a topic to discuss

2. Practice expressing your thoughts and feelings using "I" statements.

3. Switch roles and repeat the exercise with a new topic.

***   ***   ***

Should you use the word "Should?"

Using the word "should" in conversations between couples can potentially damage the relationship.

Here are some reasons why:

Implies judgment: Using the word "should" implies that there is a right or wrong way to do something. When you tell your partner what they "should" do, it can be judgmental and critical, leading to defensiveness and hurt feelings.

Creates expectations: Using the word "should" creates expectations your partner may be unable to meet. This can lead to feelings of guilt, inadequacy, and disappointment. It can also put pressure on the relationship and create unnecessary stress.

Limits options: Using the word "should" can limit your partner's choices and prevent them from exploring possible solutions or approaches to a problem. It can also create a power dynamic where one partner dictates what the other partner should do.

Disempowers your partner: Using the word "should" can make your partner feel like they are not capable of making their own decisions. It can be disempowering and undermine their confidence and self-esteem.

Instead of using this word try using more supportive and empowering language. Use "I" statements to express your feelings and needs and offer suggestions rather than demands. For example, instead of saying, "You should do this," you could say, "I would appreciate it if you considered doing this," or "What do you think about trying this?" This way, you can have a more open and collaborative conversation that respects your partner's autonomy and strengthens your relationship.

Here are some examples of using the word "should" in a relationship:

- "You should spend more time with me" - This can come across as needy or controlling and may make your partner feel suffocated or resentful.

- "You should stop hanging out with your friends so much" - This can signify jealousy or insecurity and may lead to isolation or resentment.

- "You should stop doing that; it's annoying" - This can come across as critical or judgmental and may make your partner feel unsupported.

- "We should be more like other couples" - Such comparison can signal unrealistic expectations and may lead to feelings of inadequacy or pressure.

- "You should know what I want without me having to tell you" - This can signify passive-aggressiveness or unrealistic expectations and may lead to misunderstandings or resentment.

Using the word "should" can harm a relationship, creating feelings of pressure, inadequacy, or resentment.

Change your Words, Change your Thinking, Change your Life Technology™

Saying, "You never listen, or you never understand me." will not lead to anything productive in your relationship. If you make these statements to your partner, think about how you can stop, take a break, and consider ways YOU can communicate more effectively, leading to a closer love relationship.

Conclusion

Couples communicating effectively are more likely to be satisfied with their relationship and less likely to experience relationship distress. By practicing active listening, using "I" statements, practicing empathy, honest expression, avoiding mind reading, practicing active problem solving, and taking breaks during conflicts, you can improve communication and build a deeper connection with your partner.

Poor communication can lead to misunderstandings, hurt

feelings, and resentment. In some cases, it can even lead to the breakdown of the relationship. That is why developing practical communication skills and prioritizing them in your relationship is essential.

To ensure success in your relationship, it is vital to put in the effort to continually improve your communication skills. The key is to be committed to the process and to prioritize effective communication as a foundational element of your relationship.

Remember that effective communication involves talking *and* listening, where both partners are equally committed to improving their skills. By working together and practicing regularly, you can build a relationship based on trust, understanding, and mutual respect. Use the exercises provided in this chapter to practice these skills, and watch as your relationship flourishes.

♥♥

CHAPTER 4: TRUST: THE FOUNDATION FOR LASTING LOVE

Trust is essential for any healthy relationship, but it can be fragile, easily damaged, and eroded by dishonesty, broken promises, and infidelity. Trust is not something that happens instantaneously. Trust is earned over time by experiencing repeated trusting behaviors without trust-damaging actions.

This chapter examines the different dimensions of trust, including:

- **Reliability**
- **Honesty**
- **Vulnerability**

It also gives guidance for building and supporting trust in a relationship. We will cover topics such as:

- **Forgiveness**
- **Transparency**
- **Consistency**

Then we will look at evidence-based strategies for repairing broken trust. This chapter also explores the role of self-trust in relationships and how cultivating a powerful sense of self-worth and self-esteem can improve your ability to trust and be trusted by others.

PRO TIP

When you start dating someone, talk to the friends of your potential partner. Ask about how trustworthy that person has been over time.

The Importance of Trust

Trust is the foundation of all successful relationships. It is the belief that your partner is believable, reliable, and has your best interests at heart. Trust enables you to feel safe, secure, and comfortable in your relationship, and it is essential for building intimacy.

When trust is present in a relationship, it fosters open communication, honesty, and vulnerability. Trust also enables couples to share their deepest fears, desires, and insecurities without fear of judgment, criticism, or rejection. Trust also enables partners to rely on one another, support each other during challenging times, and helps them make important decisions together.

Trust is linked to emotional and physical intimacy. Couples who trust each other are more likely to feel secure, connected, and satisfied. However, trust is not something that is automatically granted in a relationship. It must be earned through consistent behavior over time. Trust can also be easily eroded if one partner acts in a way inconsistent with the other partner's expectations or values. Lying, being unfaithful and other forms of betrayal can shatter even the most robust relationships. However, it is possible to rebuild trust over time if both partners are willing to work at it.

Factors that Erode Trust

Several factors can erode trust in a relationship. These include:

Dishonesty: Dishonesty, whether overtly or covertly, is one of the most significant factors that can erode trust in a relationship.

Infidelity: Whether physical or emotional, infidelity can devastate a relationship and damage trust.

Broken promises: A partner who consistently fails to follow through on commitments can erode trust, leading to disappointment and resentment.

Lack of communication: When partners do not communicate or are unclear when they do, this can lead to misunderstandings and wear down trust over time.

Lack of reliability: When a partner consistently fails to be dependable, whether it is showing up on time or following through on commitments, it can lead to feelings of disappointment and frustration. Fortunately, trust can be built and supported through consistent effort and positive behaviors.

PRO TIP

Honesty is the cornerstone of trust. It is essential to be upfront with your partner, even though discussing your feelings, needs, and boundaries might be difficult. Couples communicating honestly are more satisfied with their relationships and enjoy greater trust.

Exercise

Practice "radical honesty" with your partner by sharing something requiring vulnerability that you have been holding back. This could be a fear, regret, or desire you have hesitated to share. Give your partner the opportunity to respond with empathy and support.

Example

Chris and Sam struggled with trust issues after Chris had an emotional affair with a coworker. They collaborated with a therapist to rebuild trust by practicing radical honesty, setting clear boundaries, and checking in regularly about their feelings and needs.

Tips for Building and Maintaining Trust

Being transparent, reliable, and vulnerable with your partner is essential to build and foster trust.

Be Honest: Honesty is the cornerstone of trust. Be honest with your partner, even when difficult, and avoid hiding or omitting information. Subterfuge in a relationship is terminal.

Communicate Openly: Open and honest communication is essential for building trust. Be willing to share your headaches and joys with your partner and listen actively when they are communicating with you.

Follow Through on Commitments: Following through on commitments, both big and small, shows reliability and builds trust over time. If you make a promise, follow through on it.

This includes minor things like picking up groceries on the way home and large commitments like being faithful.

Be Consistent: Consistency is vital in building and maintaining trust. Ensure your actions and behaviors are consistent with your words and commitments.

Show Empathy: Empathy is understanding and sharing your partner's feelings. Showing empathy demonstrates you care about their emotions and fosters a deeper connection and trust.

Additional Exercises to Build and Maintain Trust

The Trust-Building Exercise

The Trust-Building Exercise involves making and keeping small promises to each other over time. This exercise helps to show reliability.

The Alchemy of Affection

To do the Trust-Building Exercise:

Make a small promise to your partner that you can keep easily, such as doing the dishes after dinner.

Follow through on the promise.

After successfully keeping the promise, ask your significant other to make a small promise to you.

Continue making and keeping small promises with each other over time to build trust and reliability.

The Appreciation Exercise

The Appreciation Exercise involves expressing appreciation for your partner. This exercise helps to build trust by fostering positive emotions and reinforcing the connection between partners.

To do the Appreciation Exercise:

Take turns expressing appreciation for each other.

Focus on specific actions that your significant other has done that you appreciate.

Express Your Appreciation Genuinely

Here are some tips to help you express your appreciation genuinely:

Be specific: Instead of offering a general "thank you," mention specific details about what you appreciate. For example, you can say, "I appreciate your taking the time to listen to me and offer valuable advice. It meant a lot to me."

Use sincere language: Choose your words carefully and speak from the heart. Express your gratitude in a way that feels authentic to you. Avoid clichés or generic phrases and instead focus on expressing your genuine emotions.

Be present and attentive: When expressing appreciation, give your full attention to the person you're thanking. Maintain eye contact, use their name, and show genuine interest in what you're saying. Your body language and demeanor should reflect your sincerity.

Share the impact: Explain how the person's actions or words affected you. Tell them how their kindness, support, or assistance made a difference in your life. This shows that you genuinely value their contributions.

Write a thoughtful note: If you find it difficult to express your appreciation verbally, consider writing a heartfelt message. This gives you time to choose your words and express your gratitude more composedly and carefully.

Offer help in return: Sometimes, the best way to show your appreciation is by reciprocating the kindness or support you received. Let the person know you are available to help them in any way you can.

Be genuine and authentic: Above all, be true to yourself. Express your appreciation in a way that reflects your personality and feelings. People often sense authenticity, and genuine gratitude will have a more profound impact.

Remember, genuine appreciation is about acknowledging the other person's contribution, showing gratitude from the heart, and making them feel valued.

***   ***   ***

The Forgiveness Exercise

The Forgiveness Exercise involves practicing forgiveness for past hurt or transgressions. This exercise helps to build trust by enabling couples to move past injuries and make a stronger connection.

<u>To do the Forgiveness Exercise:</u>

Sit down with your partner and discuss any past hurts or transgressions. Practice forgiveness by acknowledging the pain, expressing empathy, and offering forgiveness. Commit to overcoming hurt and working together to build a stronger relationship.

Examples

Jenna and Adam

Jenna and Adam had been together for several years when she discovered that he had been keeping a secret from her. At first, Jenna was angry and hurt, and she struggled to trust Adam again. However, Adam was committed to rebuilding Jenna's trust and worked hard to follow through on his promises and communicate openly and honestly with her. They practiced the Trust-Building and Forgiveness Exercises and committed to working on their relationship. Over time, Jenna could trust Adam again, and they built a stronger connection and a more profound love.

Sarah and Avery

Another couple, Sarah and Avery, needed help with communication and reliability in their relationship. Avery often forgot to follow through on commitments, which frustrated and disappointed Sarah. However, he was committed to making changes and worked hard to be more reliable and communicative with Sarah. They practiced the Trust-Building and Appreciation Exercises, and Sarah tried to express her appreciation for Avery's efforts. Over time, they built a stronger foundation of trust and communication in their relationship.

More Exercises to Build Trust

Practice active listening: Set aside 10-15 minutes each day to practice active listening with your partner. This means giving them your full attention, asking clear and even probing questions, and reflecting on your partner's words.

Write down your commitments: Putting commitments into writing makes the statements more real. When you are ready, share this text with your significant other. Refer to this list regularly to remind yourself of your promises.

*** *** ***

The Vulnerability Exercise

The Vulnerability Exercise involves sharing your fears, hopes, and dreams with your partner. This exercise helps build trust by allowing partners to be vulnerable and deepen their emotional connection.

To do the Vulnerability Exercise:

Set aside time to sit with your partner and talk openly and honestly about your feelings. Share your fears, hopes, and dreams. Take turns sharing your fears and insecurities. This can help to build intimacy and trust by showing vulnerability and allowing your partner to support and reassure you.

The Honesty Exercise

The Honesty Exercise involves being forthright when communicating with your partner. This exercise helps to build trust by fostering honest communication.

<u>To do the Honesty Exercise:</u>

Commit to being honest with your partner. Practice active listening and open communication. Be willing to admit when you are wrong or have made a mistake.

Examples

Tom and Emily

Tom and Emily had been together for several years when they started to notice a lack of trust in their relationship. She had been feeling insecure and was struggling to trust Tom, who had a history of infidelity in past relationships. However, Tom was committed to being transparent with Emily and worked hard to rebuild her trust. They practiced the Honesty Exercise, where Tom committed to being truthful with Emily and avoiding situations that could lead to temptation. They also practiced the Vulnerability Exercise, where they shared their fears and hopes with each other, and the Boundaries Exercise, where they established clear guidelines for behavior and communication. Over time, their relationship improved, and they built a more robust connection based on trust and honesty.

Lisa and Jack

Lisa and Jack had been together for several years, but Lisa had always struggled with trust issues. Jack knew that he needed to be patient and consistent in his actions to earn Lisa's trust. He made a conscious effort to be transparent about his whereabouts and communicate openly and honestly about his feelings. Over time, Lisa began to feel more secure in the relationship, and their bond deepened.

***   ***   ***

Types of Boundaries to Consider for Your Relationship

Time boundaries: You might set boundaries around how much time you spend together versus apart. For example, you might agree to have designated "me time" or "friend time" to pursue individual hobbies or hang out with friends.

Communication boundaries: You might set boundaries around how you communicate with each other. For example, you might agree to avoid yelling or name-calling during arguments or decide not to bring up specific topics you know will lead to conflict.

Physical boundaries: You might set boundaries around physical touch or affection. For example, you might agree on what kinds of physical contact are acceptable in public versus private settings and when you are out by yourself interacting with friends.

Sexual boundaries: You might also discuss your sexual boundaries. Think about what you are comfortable with and what would push you out of your comfort zone.

Financial boundaries: You might want to set boundaries around your finances, such as how you both spend money, how you split bills and expenses, or how you handle debt.

Social media boundaries: You might set boundaries around what is acceptable and what is not regarding spending time, following others online, posting videos of your relationship, or flirting with others online.. By doing so, couples can enjoy the benefits of social media while maintaining a healthy and loving relationship.

Social boundaries: You might set boundaries around your social lives, such as how often you go out with friends or how you act at social events as a couple.

Personal boundaries: You might set boundaries around personal issues like mental health or family dynamics. For example, you might agree to respect each other's need for space or privacy when dealing with specific emotional problems or triggering family issues.

*** *** ***

The Boundaries Exercise

The Boundaries Exercise involves setting clear boundaries and expectations in your relationship. This exercise helps to build trust by establishing clear guidelines for behavior and communication.

To do the Boundaries Exercise:
- Sit down with your partner and discuss your boundaries and expectations.
- Make sure that your boundaries and expectations are realistic and achievable.
- Practice respecting each other's boundaries and expectations.

Couples Putting Boundaries Into Statements

- "I need some alone time to recharge. Can we agree to set aside a few hours each week where I can have some time to myself?"
- "I understand you might have a different opinion than I do, but we must try to avoid using hurtful language."
- "I love physical touch, but I feel uncomfortable with public displays of affection. Can we agree to save our physical touch for when we are alone?"
- "I'd like to talk about how we handle our finances. Can we sit down and come up with a plan that works for both of us?"
- "I enjoy spending time with our friends but also need some alone time with you. Can we spend one night a week together without any other obligations?"
- "I'm dealing with some personal issues I'm not ready to share yet. Can we agree to give each other space and support when I'm ready to talk?"

In each statement, the speaker expresses their need for a boundary clearly and respectfully, suggesting how they can work together to honor that boundary. By using "I" statements and focusing on their needs and feelings, the speaker avoids blame or judgment and opens up a space for honest communication and compromise.

Example

Rachel and Jan

Rachel and Jan had been together for several years and had a strong connection based on a love of animals, travel, and their church. However, they needed help with communication and boundary-setting. They often got caught up in their individual pursuits and did not make time for each other. They were committed to improving their relationship and practiced the Boundaries Exercise, where they set clear expectations for communication and quality time. They also practiced the Vulnerability Exercise, where they shared their fears and hopes with each other, and the Honesty Exercise, where they committed to being transparent in their communication.

Incorporating these exercises into your daily routine can help improve trust and intimacy in your relationship. Additionally, it is essential to remember that trust must be reciprocal. **Both partners** must be committed to building trust and improving their relationship. Both partners must be willing to put in the effort to make the relationship stronger.

PRO TIP

If you are struggling to build trust in your relationship, consider seeking the help of a professional. A couples therapist can provide tools and techniques to improve your relationship and build confidence. Additionally, they can help you work through any issues preventing you from building trust.

Change your Words, Change your Thinking, Change your Life Technology™

If your trust has been broken, saying, "I will never trust you again," will become prophetic. Instead, consider saying, "It will be hard for me to trust again." Which leaves open the door to working on your relationship. We may desire perfection from our partner, and it is essential to recognize that their imperfections can sometimes hurt or affect us. However, it is also crucial to remain open to the possibility of growth and improvement, giving our partner a chance to learn and develop even if they have not mastered some of the essential relationship skills.

It is also important to remember that trust is built over time. It takes time, effort, and patience. If you have experienced a breach of confidence in your relationship, it is natural to feel hurt and angry. It is essential to give yourself time to heal and work through any issues that may arise.

Conclusion

Trust is vital for building a healthy and loving relationship. It enables our partner to feel safe, secure, and connected and is essential for building intimacy and closeness. Following the tips and exercises outlined in this chapter, you can create and maintain trust in your relationship and foster a deeper, more loving connection with your significant other. Building trust takes time and effort, but the rewards are worth it.

Part II: The Alchemy of Healing and Transformation

CHAPTER 5: REMOVING BARRIERS TO LOVE

Our primary emphasis will now be on nurturing intimacy as a fundamental aspect of a lasting and loving relationship. We will identify and eliminate any obstacles hindering the growth of intimacy, creating an environment where it can thrive and flourish.

Maintaining healthy intimacy in a relationship can be difficult, but it is essential for a long-lasting, fulfilling partnership. In this chapter, we will explore the various types of intimacy, including emotional, physical, and spiritual, and provide tips for cultivating and deepening each.

Additionally, we'll address common obstacles that hinder intimacy, such as communication issues, trust concerns, and unresolved conflicts. Drawing on insights from Attachment Theory as well as Positive Psychology, we will offer practical strategies for building intimacy and connection with your partner.

Communication

Communication is the foundation of any relationship and **is essential to achieving intimacy**. However, many couples have communication problems, which can hinder their ability to connect on a deeper level.

Tools for Building Communication Intimacy

Practice active listening: As has been mentioned earlier in this book, to cultivate a strong and healthy relationship, it's important to practice active listening. This involves fully engaging in the conversation, refraining from interrupting, and repeating what your partner says to ensure complete understanding before responding.

Throughout this book, active listening has been emphasized as a critical skill for fostering love and connection with your partner. By mastering this skill, you can deepen your understanding of each other and build a stronger foundation for your relationship.

Avoid making assumptions: Instead of assuming you know what your partner means, ask for clarification to avoid misunderstandings.

Express yourself honestly: It is essential to express your true feelings and desires in a non-judgmental way so your partner can understand you more deeply.

Trust Blockages

Trust is the foundation of any strong, intimate relationship. Without it, couples can struggle to connect on a deeper level. Trust issues can arise from experience or current behavior, leading one or both partners to feel guarded. As a result, building and maintaining trust is crucial for developing a lasting and fulfilling connection with your partner.

Trust is a crucial element in any intimate relationship. When one partner has trust issues owing to infidelity or past negative experiences, it can lead to suspicion and jealousy, creating a barrier to intimacy. Similarly, lying or keeping secrets from your partner can erode trust and cause mistrust to fester. Failing to keep your promises can also contribute to mistrust and create distance in a relationship.

More Tools for Building Intimacy

Be honest and transparent: Being transparent about your actions and intentions can help build and maintain trust.

Take responsibility for your actions: If you have broken your partner's trust, own up to it and work to repair the damage.

Follow through on commitments: Consistency is vital; following through on promises can help build trust over time.

***   ***   ***

Unresolved Conflicts

Unresolved conflicts can be detrimental to the health of a relationship, causing tension and emotional distance. It is essential to address disagreements promptly and effectively to maintain intimacy and connection. (Conflicts are discussed in more detail in the next chapter.)

Even More Tools for Building Intimacy

Address conflicts promptly: Don't avoid conflict or let issues fester. Address them as soon as possible to prevent them from building up while at the same time giving yourself a chance to cool down in the heat of the moment.

Use "I" statements: Instead of blaming or attacking your partner, use "I" statements to express how their actions or words made you feel.

Work together to find a solution: Instead of trying to win the battle, work together to find a solution that works for both partners, which often includes compromising.

Triggers

The next step in building intimacy is to discuss and identify ways to address triggers.

A relationship trigger is an event, situation, or behavior that evokes an emotional response in one or both partners. Triggers can be positive or negative and can be related to the past, current stressors, or specific behaviors. *Triggers can be anything that causes a strong emotional response, such as a certain tone of voice, a particular behavior, or a specific situation.*

For example, if one partner has been cheated on in the past, hearing their current partner talking with an ex may trigger feelings of jealousy and insecurity. Alternatively, if one partner is stressed at work, their person's minor mistake or forgetfulness may trigger an overreaction or anger. Identifying and addressing relationship triggers can bolster communication, build trust, and strengthen the relationship overall.

Another critical aspect of managing triggers is understanding and respecting each other's boundaries. Each partner has unique needs and limits, and it is essential to communicate and honor these boundaries in the relationship. For example, if one partner needs alone time to recharge, the other needs to respect that and not take it personally.

Keep your individuality

In any relationship, it is important to prioritize self-care and maintain our identities. This means taking care of oneself physically and mentally, pursuing hobbies and interests, and spending time with friends and family outside of the relationship. By maintaining a sense of self and investing in personal growth, individuals can bring their best selves to the relationship and avoid becoming overly reliant on their partner for happiness and fulfillment.

Additional Tips and Exercises to Help You Build Intimacy

Identify your triggers: Take time to reflect on situations or behaviors that trigger negative emotions or reactions. Write them down and share them with your partner.

Discuss and find solutions: For each trigger, work together to find ways to address it constructively. Brainstorm strategies and agree on a plan of action.

Example

Shikira found herself in a precarious situation due to an emotional trigger that hijacked her rationality. As she walked into a crowded room, the sight of her ex-boyfriend engaged in a lively conversation with an attractive woman ignited a surge of jealousy and insecurity within her. Overwhelmed by these intense emotions, Shikira's judgment became clouded, and without thinking, she impulsively confronted her ex-boyfriend, unleashing a wave of accusations and hurtful words. The atmosphere in the room grew tense as bystanders witnessed the escalation of a once-harmless encounter into a volatile exchange. At that moment, Shikira realized the destructive power of emotional triggers and the dire consequences they can entail, leaving her to grapple with the aftermath of her impulsive actions.

Change your Words, Change your Thinking, Change your Life Technology™

When you **understand** the words or actions that trigger your partner and, more importantly, the words or actions that trigger an emotional response in yourself, you can recognize this response, which is the first step in making a healthy change.

PRO TIP

Ask for Help. Remember, building a healthy relationship is an ongoing process that requires constant attention and effort. If you are struggling in your relationship, do not be afraid to seek help from a therapist. With the proper guidance and support, you can overcome obstacles and build a strong, loving relationship.

It is crucial to manage triggers to build and maintain a healthy relationship. Understanding the triggers that affect us and our partner can help us communicate more effectively, respect boundaries, and build a strong foundation of trust and intimacy. While confronting and working through triggers can be challenging, the effort is well worth it. Couples can overcome their triggers with practice and commitment, and in doing so, they can build a lasting, fulfilling relationship free from unnecessary conflicts and misunderstandings.

Triggers Can Be Tricky

In dealing with triggers in particular, it can be especially helpful to have a third party such as a therapist to help you through this forest of emotions.

Here Are Some Factors to Consider When Choosing a Couples Therapist

Qualifications and credentials: Make sure the therapist is licensed to practice and has training and experience in couples therapy. Feel free to ask about their credentials and google their meanings.

Availability and location: Consider the therapist's availability and location, as well as their hours and fees.

Specialization: Consider their specializations. Some therapists may specialize in particular issues or populations, such as infidelity or LGBTQ+ couples.

Referrals: Ask for referrals from trusted sources, such as your doctor or friends who have had successful therapeutic experiences.

Compatibility: Choose a therapist you both feel comfortable with and believe can effectively help you work through your issues. You are the expert when it comes to your instinct. Talk with a few therapists on the phone and ask questions. One will stand above the rest.

Reviews: Look for websites that offer reviews of couples therapists in your area. You can look at Yelp or Google by searching "reviews of couples therapists in my area."

Phone calls: Take a few minutes to speak with at least three couples therapists on the phone. Each counselor should be willing to take a few minutes to talk generally about the issues you are facing and then state whether they feel comfortable working with these issues. Your reaction to this initial call will give you a feeling about who to start seeing. The cost is worth your peace of mind and growth.

Approach to therapy: Therapists have different approaches to couples therapy. Choosing one whose approach and style align with your needs and preferences is important.

Approaches Used by Couples Therapists

Here are some common approaches used by therapists that work well for individuals but also for couples:

Emotionally Focused Therapy (EFT): EFT is a type of therapy that aims to help couples identify and understand their emotions and how they affect their relationship. The therapist helps the couple recognize and express their feelings in a safe and supportive environment and then works with them to develop new communication and behavior patterns.

Cognitive Behavioral Therapy (CBT): CBT is a type of therapy that focuses on identifying and changing negative patterns of thought and behavior. In couples therapy, the therapist may help the couple to recognize negative patterns in their communication or behavior and then work with them to develop new, more positive patterns.

The Gottman Method: The Gottman Method is a research-based approach to couples therapy that focuses on building stronger relationships through communication, conflict resolution, and shared goals. The therapist uses various techniques to help the couple improve their communication and build a stronger connection.

Solution-Focused Therapy: Solution-focused therapy focuses on helping the couple identify and achieve specific goals. The therapist helps the couple to identify their strengths and resources and then works with them to develop a plan to achieve their goals.

Imago Therapy: Imago couples therapy helps couples to identify their childhood wounds and to learn how to communicate and respond to each other in a more loving and compassionate way. The therapy also teaches couples how to resolve conflict in a healthy and productive way.

Narrative Therapy: Narrative therapy focuses on helping the couple create a new narrative about their relationship. The therapist helps the couple identify negative patterns of thought and behavior and then works with them to create a new story emphasizing the positive aspects of their relationship.

Psychodynamic therapy: This approach focuses on understanding the unconscious factors that may be contributing to relationship problems.

The approach used by a couples therapist may vary depending on the couple's specific needs. The therapist may use a combination of different techniques and approaches to help the couple improve their relationship and achieve their goals. If you feel moved by the description of one type of therapy listed above, seek a counselor trained in that mode of assistance.

PRO TIP

If your partner will not go to couples counseling, which is common, then go by yourself to learn how to interact more healthily in your relationship. Your positive experience may demonstrate the value and then your partner may decide to join you.

Overall, taking the time to research and choose the right couples therapist can greatly increase the chances of a successful therapy outcome. You do not have to continue with the first counselor you visit. Go with your instincts. If you do not feel this person is a good fit for you or your relationship, move on to another.

Premarital Counseling and its Usefulness For Your Relationship

In our society, marriage is considered by many to be the ultimate commitment. Many couples find premarital counseling helpful. To better understand how premarital counseling can enhance your relationship, let's explore its purpose and the benefits it offers for strengthening your bond whether or not you are getting married.

The top ten topics covered in premarital counseling are:
1. Communication
2. Conflict resolution
3. Financial management
4. Intimacy and sexual expectations
5. Family dynamics and expectations
6. Roles and responsibilities
7. Children and Parenting
8. Religion and spirituality
9. Emotional health and well-being
10. Expectations and goals for the marriage

Discussing these topics during premarital counseling helps couples better understand their relationship, the challenges they may face in the future, and offer constructive ways to navigate all of it in a positive and loving way.

PRO TIP

Premarital counseling can be transformative for couples because it can help them identify potential issues and strengthen their relationship before marriage. By discussing topics such as communication, finances, values, and expectations, couples can better understand each other's perspectives and work through any challenges that may arise. It's never too early to start working on your relationship and investing in your future together.

Benefits of Counseling

Conflict resolution: Conflicts are inevitable in any relationship, but how couples navigate and address them can significantly impact the long-term sustainability of their bond. In counseling, couples can learn conflict resolution skills and strategies to handle disagreements in a healthy and respectful manner.

Financial management: Counseling can help couples develop a plan for managing finances and discuss their financial expectations and goals.

Intimacy and sexual expectations: Counseling can provide a safe space for couples to discuss their sexual expectations and concerns about intimacy.

Family dynamics and expectations: Counseling can help couples explore their family histories and expectations and how they may affect their relationship. This includes how relatives will influence your relationship.

Roles and responsibilities: In any relationship, it is essential to establish roles and responsibilities. Counseling can help couples discuss their expectations and agree on how they will manage their household and other responsibilities.

Children and parenting: If a couple plans to have children, discussing parenting styles and expectations is essential. Counseling can help couples explore their views on parenting and establish a plan for how they will raise their children.

Religion and spirituality: Counseling can provide a space for couples to discuss their beliefs and explore how they will incorporate them into their relationship.

Expectations and goals for marriage: Counseling can help couples explore their expectations and establish a plan for achieving their goals.

*** *** ***

How well do you know your partner? Have you discussed all of the topics above? Even if you are not getting married, these can be useful for uncovering topics for discussion that are bound to arise in your long-term love relationship.

Couples can establish a relationship with a therapist before any major issues develop. This can help both of you to feel more comfortable discussing sensitive topics. This can also help the therapist better understand your couples dynamic and provide more targeted guidance and support.

♥♥

CHAPTER 6: CONFLICT: TURNING CHALLENGES INTO GROWTH

Every relationship is bound to face conflicts. How couples navigate and resolve them determines the strength of their bond. This chapter explores the disputes that can arise in relationships, from communication breakdowns to differences in values and power struggles. By offering real-world strategies for resolving conflicts with compassion and empathy, you can develop the skills to navigate these complicated situations constructively. This chapter also highlights the role of self-awareness and mindfulness practices in conflict resolution, illustrating how they can help you stay engaged in challenging conversations. By mastering these skills, you can build stronger and more resilient relationships, deepen your understanding of your partner, and ultimately create a more profound sense of trust and connection.

Transforming an unhealthy relationship takes effort because it requires understanding your fears, desires, and shortcomings…and then putting someone else first.

The Science of Conflict

Conflict triggers the fight or flight response in the brain, flooding our bodies with adrenaline and cortisol. These stress hormones can impact our ability to think clearly and make rational decisions, making it harder to resolve conflicts effectively. However, conflict can also activate the release of oxytocin, the "love hormone," which can increase feelings of trust and connection between partners.

Couples who reported high conflict resolution skills were also more likely to report elevated levels of relationship satisfaction. Learning how to manage conflict in a healthy way can have a significant impact on the overall quality of your relationship.

Practical Tips for Handling Conflict

Take a Time-Out: When conflict arises, taking a step back and giving yourself time to cool off is essential. This will help you avoid saying or doing things you regret and enable you to collect your thoughts and emotions. Make sure your partner understands you are only taking a short break and will return to work through the issue.

Practice Active Listening: Active listening involves fully engaging with your partner and trying to understand their perspective without interrupting or judging them. This can reduce defensiveness and promote a more collaborative approach to conflict resolution.

Use "I" Statements: When expressing your feelings, it is essential to use "I" statements instead of "you" statements. For example, instead of saying, "You always do this," try saying, "I feel hurt when this happens."

Compromise: Finding a solution for both partners is crucial in resolving conflicts. Compromising and finding a middle ground helps maintain a sense of fairness and mutual respect in the relationship.

Counseling: Seeking the help of a trained therapist can be beneficial for couples struggling to resolve conflicts on their own. A therapist can provide guidance on how to communicate effectively, identify underlying issues, and develop strategies to resolve disputes in a healthy and productive manner.

How Couples Can Compromise With Each Other

Be open to different perspectives: Try to understand your partner's point of view, even if you don't agree with it. Listen actively and ask questions to gain a deeper understanding of their perspective.

Find common ground: Look for areas where you both agree or where there is room for compromise. Identify what is most important to each of you and find ways to meet in the middle.

Brainstorm options: Brainstorm together to come up with workable solutions that can meet both of your needs. Write down all the options and evaluate each to see which works best for both of you.

Be flexible: Be willing to be flexible and adjust as needed. Be open to trying new things and be ready to change your expectations if necessary.

Make trade-offs: Compromise involves making trade-offs. For example, if one partner wants to take a vacation while the other wants to save money, they could compromise by planning a more affordable vacation or postponing the trip until they have saved enough money.

Set clear expectations: Be clear about what you are willing to compromise on versus what is non-negotiable. This can help avoid misunderstandings and ensure that both partners are in sync.

Keep the focus on the relationship: Remember that compromise is about finding a solution that works for both of you and strengthens the connection. Focus on the relationship and work together to find a solution that benefits both of you.

PRO TIP

Having an insightful couples counselor can be a valuable asset in nurturing the growth and flourishing of your relationship, regardless of whether or not you are currently facing issues. Relationships inevitably encounter challenges, and having a trusted professional to turn to when you find yourself stuck can provide invaluable support. By being proactive and actively working to strengthen your relationship, you can enhance its depth and fulfillment. Seeking guidance and support does not have to be reserved for times of crisis or distress. Instead, consider it a proactive step towards fostering a resilient and thriving partnership. Embracing the guidance of a couples counselor can empower you with the tools and insights necessary to navigate potential obstacles and cultivate a deeper connection with your partner. Together, you can embark on a journey of growth, continuously nurturing your relationship to reach new heights of love and fulfillment.

Maria and James

Maria and James had been dating for six months when they had their first major fight. James had made plans to go out with his friends on Maria's birthday, which made her feel neglected. At first, they both became defensive and angry, but eventually, they could step back and listen to each other's perspectives. They realized that James had assumed Maria would want to spend her birthday with her friends and family and had never considered how his plans might make her feel. By talking through their feelings and finding commonality, they were able to turn the conflict into an opportunity for growth and understanding.

Exercises For Conflict Resolution

Role Play: Take turns practicing conflict resolution with your partner through role-playing before you actually have a problem. If you are feeling confident, you could try working through an issue that has come up in your past, but you will have the most success doing this with a couples therapist present.

Write your thoughts: Writing a letter or text can be a great way to express yourself if you are having trouble communicating your thoughts and feelings to your partner. By putting your thoughts down on paper, you can organize your ideas and emotions in a clear and concise way. Additionally, writing can help you process your feelings and gain greater insight into your perspective.

However, it's important to note that written communication can also be misinterpreted, so it's essential to take the time to carefully consider your words and phrasing. Before sending the letter or text, review it to ensure it conveys your intended message, and consider seeking feedback from a trusted friend or family member. Also, let it sit for a while then return to it with a fresh perspective.

When sharing your written thoughts with your partner, it can be helpful to do so in person. This enables you to have a conversation about your feelings and enables your partner to ask questions or seek clarification.

Change your Words, Change your Thinking, Change your Life Technology™

Do not believe it when you hear about couples having a great relationship without issues. All couples have struggles and issues to work through. If they don't have some struggles, then they don't have a deep connection that has been forged with effort. If you accept that all couples have issues, it is easier to accept that you can be one of the successful couples seeking help through a book like this or with a professional couples counselor.

Conflict and Support

When you are struggling, it is easy to vent with friends and family but remember you also want them to hear about your positive times. You want these people to support your relationship.

Hurtful Words

Communication in relationships ought always aim to be respectful, honest, and constructive. Using hurtful words can cause irreparable damage to the relationship and may not be easy to take back.

This is a list of statements to avoid saying to your partner. You cannot easily take these back and they can cause hurt for a long time. This is not an exhaustive list. It is to give you an idea that words can hurt deeply. So be careful with what you say.

Here are some examples of hurtful things that couples might say to each other:

- You're not good enough for me
- I wish I had never met you
- I'm ashamed to be seen with you
- You're just like your [negative family member]
- You are so stupid

The Alchemy of Affection

- You are a terrible lover
- You're never going to change
- I'm only staying with you for the kids
- I'm not attracted to you anymore
- I wish I never married you
- You're the reason our relationship is failing
- You are fat and ugly
- You are not as attractive as X
- You're a disappointment
- You're just like your ex
- You're the worst thing that's ever happened to me

Remember, healthy communication in relationships involves constructively expressing your feelings and concerns, using "I" statements instead of "you" statements, and actively listening to your partner's perspective. If you are tempted to say something hurtful to your partner, take a step back and reflect on what you want to achieve in the conversation. It's better to take a break and cool down than to say something you may regret later.

Again, it is essential to communicate with your partner in a healthy and respectful manner. Hurtful words can cause lasting damage to your relationship and can be difficult to take back, even if you apologize later. Think about how these statements would feel to hear from your partner. Probably one or two stick out to you in a painful way. Remember what it would feel like to listen to these statements said to you, so you can do your best not to say hurtful things.

Fighting Fair

Fighting fair in a relationship means expressing your feelings and concerns using "I statements" without attacking your partner and actively listening to your partner's perspective without interrupting or belittling them.

Here is an Example of Not Fighting Fair in a Relationship

Let us say that a couple is arguing about managing a difficult situation at work. One partner becomes defensive and angry and starts attacking the other partner by saying things like: "You always mess things up! I can't believe I have to deal with your incompetence! Why can't you be more like me?"

The other partner may respond by becoming defensive or angry themselves, and the argument quickly becomes a shouting match, with both partners saying hurtful things to each other.

This kind of argument is not fighting fair because it involves personal attacks, blaming, and belittling rather than focusing on the underlying issue and respectfully expressing feelings. It can cause both partners to feel hurt, disrespected, and unheard, damaging the trust and intimacy in the relationship.

To fight fair, it is important to avoid attacking your partner and instead focus on the issue at hand. This involves expressing your feelings and concerns using "I" statements, actively listening to your person's perspective, and working together to find a solution that works for both of you.

Here is an Example Of Fighting Fair in a Relationship
Imagine one partner feels frustrated owing to the other partner's consistent lateness. Instead of resorting to yelling or placing blame, the partner can communicate their emotions by saying, "I feel upset when you're consistently late because it gives me the impression that my time isn't valued. Can we collaborate to find a solution that addresses this issue in a way that benefits both of us?"

The other partner can respond by actively listening, seeking to understand their partner's perspective, and expressing their own feelings without becoming defensive or angry. For instance, they could say, "I understand why you feel upset, and I apologize for causing you to stress with my lateness. I've been struggling with managing my time effectively, but I'm committed to finding a resolution that enables us to feel respected and valued in our relationship."

By expressing their feelings honestly and respectfully, and actively listening to each other's concerns, the couple can work together to find a solution that addresses the underlying issue or issues and strengthens their relationship.

Social Media and Your Relationship

While social media can be a fun way to stay in touch with friends and family, it also can create problems for couples in long-term relationships. One of the ways is through jealousy and insecurity. When one partner sees their significant other interacting with others online, they may feel insecure about their relationship. This can be especially true if one partner frequently comments or likes the posts of someone or is following or being followed by a person with whom their partner is uncomfortable. Social media can also create problems for couples if one partner spends too much time on a particular platform. If one partner constantly checks their feed or responds to messages, it can take away from the time they could spend with their significant other. This can lead to feelings of neglect and resentment. Another way that being online can create problems for couples is through privacy concerns. If one partner shares too much information about their relationship, it can lead to disagreements and hurt feelings. For example, if one partner shares a private moment or argument online, the other may feel betrayed and embarrassed.

Any social media platform that enables users to share photos and videos with their followers can also create problems for couples if it leads to unrealistic expectations. Most online video platforms often have filtered images of perfect bodies, luxurious vacations, and idealized relationships. This can pressure couples to present an ideal image of themselves, which can be challenging if not impossible to maintain in real life. It can also lead to feelings of inadequacy if couples feel their relationship is not living up to these idealized relationships they see online.

Finally, social media can create problems for couples if it becomes a platform for emotional affairs. If one partner spends a lot of time messaging or chatting with someone online, it can lead to emotional infidelity… which can then lead to physical infidelity. This can be especially true if the person on the other end is an ex-partner or someone with whom the significant other is uncomfortable.

To avoid these problems, couples can communicate openly about their social media use and set boundaries around what is acceptable and what is not. By doing so, couples can enjoy the benefits of social media while maintaining a healthy and loving relationship.

Conclusion

Conflict is inevitable in any relationship but does not have to be negative. Using conflict as an opportunity for growth, you and your partner can strengthen your bond and build a more satisfying and fulfilling relationship. By following these practical tips and exercises, you can learn to handle conflicts in a healthy way and transform challenges into opportunities for growth and understanding.

CHAPTER 7: FORGIVENESS: HEALING WOUNDS TO STRENGTHEN YOUR BOND

Forgiveness is a conscious and intentional process of letting go of resentment, anger, and negative emotions toward one's partner for a perceived offense or wrongdoing. It involves releasing the desire for revenge or punishment and extending understanding, empathy, and compassion.

Forgiveness does not mean condoning or forgetting hurtful actions, nor does it require minimizing the offense's impact. Instead, it is a willingness to acknowledge the pain caused and actively work toward healing and reconciliation. It involves granting the other person a second chance, allowing for growth and positive change within the relationship.

Forgiveness is a transformative process that can promote emotional healing, restore harmony, and create a foundation for a stronger and more resilient bond. It allows couples to move beyond past grievances, cultivate a sense of renewal, and create a future that is not overshadowed by the weight of past transgressions.

Forgiveness is one of the most powerful tools for healing and growth in our relationships. It can also be one of the most challenging. Forgiveness requires letting go of anger, resentment, and hurt and to open ourselves to vulnerability and compassion.

The Power of Forgiveness

Forgiveness can benefit our relationships and overall well-being. It can help us reduce stress and anxiety, positively impacting our physical health. Forgiveness can also increase feelings of empathy and compassion toward our partner, improving our ability to communicate and resolve conflicts.

Additionally, forgiveness can lead to greater intimacy and trust, enabling us to let go of past hurts and evolve.

Practical Tips for Forgiveness

While forgiveness is a powerful tool, it can be challenging to achieve. Here are some helpful ways to navigate forgiveness.

Acknowledge the hurt: Acknowledging the pain caused to yourself and your partner is essential. This can help you process your emotions and begin to work toward forgiveness.

Practice empathy: Empathy is the ability to understand and share another person's feelings. Envision yourself in your partner's position when they hurt you. This does not mean condoning their actions but rather trying to understand why they acted the way they did. Then choose a situation where you have hurt someone else and try to imagine yourself in their position. Think about why they might have reacted the way they did and how your actions impacted them. This can help you gain greater compassion and understanding, leading to forgiveness.

Communicate your needs: It is essential to communicate your needs to your partner, whether it is a need for an apology, space, or reassurance. This can help you feel heard and supported in your healing process.

Ways to Move Forward

Schedule regular check-ins: Set aside time each week to check in with each other and discuss any issues in the relationship. This can prevent conflicts from escalating and enable you to address issues before they become more significant problems.

Embrace imperfection: No one is perfect, and that includes your partner. Instead of trying to change or fix their flaws, focus on accepting and loving them for who they are.

Practice self-compassion: It is essential to extend compassion not only to your partner but also to yourself. Be kind to yourself and remember that mistakes and challenges are a natural part of any relationship.

Seek support: Forgiveness can be challenging, and it is vital to seek support from friends or family. Talking about your feelings and getting an outside perspective can help you gain clarity and perspective on your situation. Your friends may want to tell you what to do but remember they do not know all aspects of your relationship and they may offer untrained advice based on their own issues.

Counseling: Couples struggling to forgive each other can benefit from therapy. A competent therapist can help you work through your issues and develop strategies for forgiveness and moving forward.

Exercises for Cultivating Forgiveness

Write a letter: Write a letter to your partner, expressing your feelings and acknowledging the pain caused. This can be a powerful tool for processing emotions and opening lines of communication. Write down their actions and how you felt. Express your desire to forgive them. This letter can be a tool to help you process your emotions and start the forgiveness process. (See later in this chapter for more details on this exercise.)

Practice gratitude: Take time each day to focus on the positive aspects of your relationship and express gratitude for what your partner does to support and love you. This can help cultivate feelings of compassion and forgiveness.

Visualize forgiveness: Try visualizing a future where you have fully forgiven your partner and can move forward in your relationship. This can help you see the benefits of forgiveness and motivate you to work toward it.

Being willing to work on forgiveness is a way of showing respect. This is for both partners. If only one side works on the forgiveness process, the relationship is not a partnership. Both individuals need to be willing to make changes and move forward for the relationship to flourish.

Keep These Additional Ideas in Mind

Self-forgiveness: Another component of healing is to practice self-forgiveness. This means reflecting on times when you may have hurt your partner and taking responsibility for your actions. It is okay not to be perfect. However, it is important to work on improving yourself. Once you have reflected on your actions, consider forgiving yourself, which can ultimately help your relationship.

Time: Forgiveness takes time, and couples are best not to rush the process. It is essential to allow time for healing and to work through any underlying issues that may have led to the situation.

Self-reflection: Each partner can take time to reflect on their behavior and how they may have contributed to the situation. By acknowledging your faults and taking responsibility for your actions, you can show your partner you are committed to making things right.

Forgiveness rituals: Some couples may find it helpful to create forgiveness rituals, such as writing a letter of apology, saying a prayer together, or performing an act of kindness for each other. This could include writing issues down and safely ripping up or burning the paper to symbolize releasing the negativity.

Show appreciation. It is essential to show your partner you appreciate them and the things they do for you. Take time to express your gratitude for the things your partner does, whether it is making dinner, doing the laundry, or simply being there for you when you need them.

Focus on the positive. When you are in a relationship, it is easy to get caught up in the negative aspects of your partner or your relationship. Instead, focus on the positive things. List what you love and appreciate about your partner and refer to it often especially when things feel difficult.

***   ***   ***

Expecting Perfection

Expecting perfection in your partner is a psychologically complicated child need-meeting feeling because when we are young, we depend on our caregivers for everything, including survival. Our survival depends on our parents' ability to meet our physical and emotional needs consistently and effectively. We feel distressed, insecure, and anxious when these needs are unmet.

As we grow older and form romantic relationships, we often transfer these expectations onto our partners. We may unconsciously expect our partners to be perfect, to always know how to meet our needs, and to never make mistakes. This can put a lot of pressure on them and lead to unrealistic expectations and disappointment.

It is essential to recognize that expecting perfection in your partner is an understandable feeling from your childhood experiences. However, it is unrealistic and awareness of this will lead to a healthier relationship.

***   ***   ***

Exercise for Cultivating Forgiveness

Create a plan for rebuilding trust

Sit down with your partner and plan how you can restore confidence in your relationship. This can include being more transparent with communication, setting clear expectations and boundaries, and demonstrating a willingness to make amends. This plan can serve as a roadmap for moving forward and rebuilding your relationship.

As mentioned earlier, using "I" statements is quite helpful here. Instead of blaming or accusing the other person, focus on expressing how you felt from their actions. For example, instead of, "You lied to me and broke my trust," say "I felt hurt and betrayed when you lied to me about where you were."

It is also essential to let go of resentment or anger toward your partner. This can be difficult but holding on to negative emotions will continue to cause harm and prevent true forgiveness.

Practice Forgiveness

No relationship is perfect, and conflicts and misunderstandings are bound to happen. Forgiving your partner and overcoming disagreements are essential for building a healthy and lasting relationship.

Forgiveness is a journey, and it will not happen overnight. It takes both people time, effort, and commitment to work toward healing and moving forward. But the benefits of forgiveness are immeasurable—greater intimacy, trust, and a deeper connection in the relationship.

Forgiveness is a powerful tool for healing wounds and finding peace in your relationship. You can cultivate a more loving and compassionate union by practicing empathy and engaging in forgiveness exercises.

In addition to these tips, you can also do exercises to help cultivate forgiveness in your relationship. One practice is to write a letter to your partner expressing your forgiveness. This letter is focused on communicating your understanding and empathy for your partner's actions and your desire to move forward with love and compassion. This can help you process your emotions and release grudges or negative feelings toward your partner.

Detailed Exercise: Writing A Forgiveness Letter

1. Begin by finding a quiet and comfortable place where you will not be disturbed. You can do this exercise alone or with your partner.

2. Write a letter to your partner expressing how you feel about the situation that caused you pain. Be specific and honest about how their actions affected you emotionally.

3. Next, write about what you learned from the experience and what you need from your partner to move forward. This could include an apology, a change in behavior, or simply a commitment to work on the relationship.

4. End the letter with an expression of forgiveness. This does not mean you forget what happened or condone your partner's actions. It simply means you are willing to forgive them. This will help you begin the process to release your anger and resentment and move forward releasing the negative emotions.

You can decide whether or not to share the letter with your partner. If you do choose to share it, be prepared to listen to their response and be open to their perspective. Remember, forgiveness is a process that takes both partners' time, patience, and effort to heal and move forward fully.

Change your Words, Change your Thinking, Change your Life Technology™

Saying, "I forgive you" does not mean that you forget the hurt that happened. It is a part of letting it go from your life and moving forward. Trust will then need to be re-established. Remember we are all imperfect. If both partners are willing to improve the relationship, you will have a good foundation for the future.

Conclusion

Forgiveness is a powerful tool for healing wounds and finding peace in our relationships. It enables us to let go of the pain and anger caused by our partner's actions and move forward with a renewed sense of love and trust.

While it is not always easy to achieve, forgiveness can benefit our well-being and connection with our partner. We can work toward a more loving and fulfilling relationship by acknowledging the hurt, practicing empathy, communicating our needs, seeking support, and using exercises to cultivate forgiveness.

By understanding the benefits of forgiveness, practicing empathy and compassion, and committing to a process of healing and growth, you can create a strong and fulfilling relationship that will grow stronger over time.

CHAPTER 8: COMPASSION: CULTIVATING EMPATHY WITH YOUR SOULMATE

Compassion is a vital ingredient in any loving relationship. It is the ability to understand and empathize with your partner's feelings and perspectives, even when they differ from your own. Compassion helps you build deeper connections, communicate more effectively, and navigate the inevitable challenges that arise in any relationship.

Cultivating compassion in relationships is linked to higher levels of relationship satisfaction and lower levels of conflict. It is also associated with greater emotional intimacy and a stronger sense of overall well-being. So, how can you cultivate compassion in your relationship? Here are some practical tips, examples of couples using the recommendations, and exercises to get you started.

Show empathy: Empathy is understanding and sharing another person's feelings. It is an essential aspect of compassion. When your partner is upset, try to imagine how you would feel in their situation. This can help you respond with kindness and understanding.

Practice empathy: Empathy requires suspending judgment, being open-minded, and acknowledging that their experience may differ from yours. Empathy enables you to validate your partner's feelings and create a more profound connection. It does not mean you must solve your partner's problem or offer a solution.

Example

Joanna felt overwhelmed with work and family responsibilities and was short-tempered with her husband Harry. Instead of getting defensive or withdrawing, Harry practiced empathy. He asked his wife how she felt and listened without interrupting or trying to solve her problems. He validated her feelings of stress and exhaustion and offered to help with some of the tasks she was struggling with. Joanna felt heard and supported, which brought them closer together.

Exercise

Imagine a situation from your partner's perspective. How might they be feeling? What needs or desires might they have? How can you validate their experience and show support?

Tools of Compassion

Offer support: When your partner is going through a difficult time, ask how to help. Let them know you are there for them and will do whatever you can to help. This can be as simple as giving a hug or offering a cup of tea. The important thing is to let your partner know that you care.

Practice forgiveness: Forgiveness is letting go of anger, resentment, or blame toward your partner and replacing it with compassion and understanding. It is not about excusing harmful behavior or forgetting the past but rather about releasing the negative emotions that can hold you back. Everyone makes mistakes, and forgiving your partner is essential. This does not mean you overlook serious transgressions, but it does mean you can try to let go of minor grievances. (See the previous chapter on forgiveness for more details on this topic.)

Saying Sorry: Be quick to say, "I am sorry." Try to feel the meaning behind the words and understand why you are saying it and realize you are trying to improve. Your partner can look for this sign that you are trying and can acknowledge your efforts. Do not make "being right" more important than your relationship.

Practice gratitude: Gratitude is acknowledging and appreciating the positive aspects of your relationship and your partner's strengths and contributions. It helps you focus on what is going well rather than dwelling on the negatives. Gratitude fosters a sense of connection and positivity, which can help buffer against stress and conflict. It is an integral part of cultivating compassion because it enables you to focus on the uplifting aspects of your relationship. Take time each day to reflect on what you appreciate about your partner. This can be as simple as thanking them for breakfast or telling them you love them.

Examples of Couples Cultivating Compassion in Their Relationships

Ali and Toni

Ali and Toni have been married for ten years. Recently, Ali lost his job and has been feeling depressed. Toni has been offering him emotional support by listening to and encouraging him to care for himself. She has reminded him of his skills and accomplishments and helped him revise his resume. Ali has been grateful for Toni's support, and they grew closer during this challenging time.

Mark and Anika

Mark and Anika have been dating for six months. Anika has a chronic illness that sometimes prevents her from going out. Mark has shown compassion by bringing her groceries and cooking meals when she cannot leave her apartment. Mark's kindness has touched Anika; she feels more connected to him.

More Exercises for Cultivating Compassion

Compassion meditation: This meditation focuses on a

person who is suffering and how you can send them love and kindness. Sit in a comfortable position and close your eyes. Visualize your partner and imagine them happy and healthy. Then, imagine them suffering, and send them thoughts of love and kindness. Repeat this visualization several times.

Random acts of kindness: List small acts of service you can do for your partner. These could include making them breakfast in bed, leaving them a love note, or giving them a massage. Try to do one act of kindness each day.

Here are Five Ideas for Random Acts of Kindness

Surprise your partner with a romantic date night: Plan a surprise date night for your partner, complete with their favorite food, drinks, and activities. This could be a simple picnic in the park or a fancy night out at a restaurant.

Write love notes: Take time to write sweet notes to your partner and leave them around the house, where they will find them throughout the day. You could write notes expressing your love and gratitude or simply remind them of a shared happy memory.

Cook a special meal: Surprise your partner by cooking their favorite meal or trying out a new recipe you know they will love. You could even set the table with candles and flowers to create a romantic atmosphere.

Give a thoughtful gift: Surprise your partner with a thoughtful gift that shows you were thinking of them. It doesn't have to be expensive—a handmade gift or a small token of appreciation can go a long way.

Take on a chore: Do something kind for your sweetheart by taking on a chore that they usually do. This could be as simple as doing the dishes or taking out the trash, but it will show your partner you appreciate their hard work and want to help them out.

Self-Improvement

Self-improvement is essential to personal growth that can positively impact your love relationship. You can become a better partner, communicate more effectively, and build a stronger, healthier relationship with your significant other by improving yourself.

Here are some ways that couples can work on self-improvement together:

Identify areas for improvement: Take time to reflect on your own personal growth and identify areas where you could improve. This could be anything from working on your communication skills, managing your emotions better, or simply making time for self-care. Share these areas with your partner and encourage them to do the same.

Set goals: Once you have identified areas for improvement, set goals that will help you achieve your desired outcome. This could be a short-term goal like taking a communication class or a long-term goal like prioritizing self-care daily. Work to hold yourself accountable.

Be open to feedback: One of the most important aspects of self-improvement is being open to feedback. Listen to your partner's constructive criticism and take it as an opportunity to grow and improve. Remember, your partner's feedback shows they care about you and want to see you succeed.

Practice empathy and understanding: Self-improvement can be a difficult and sometimes uncomfortable process. Be patient and understanding with each other as you work through your goals. Practice empathy and support each other through setbacks and challenges.

Celebrate your progress: Celebrate your successes and progress along the way. Recognize the hard work and effort you have put in and celebrate each other's growth and achievements.

Remember, the most important aspect of self-improvement is making a commitment to continuous growth and development, both individually and as a couple.

PRO TIP

This is not a competition. Remember that both partners likely will not have the same amount of motivation for improvement. Keep an open mind and look for and verbally appreciate positive changes in your partner.

Change your Words, Change your Thinking, Change your Life Technology™

Saying things like "You should appreciate all I have done for you" can be hurtful and dismissive and may not effectively communicate the true meaning of your feelings or needs. Recognizing the differences in how you and your partner react to emotional damage can help you feel more compassionate toward your partner. Many people assume that what makes them feel a certain way also will make their partner feel that way. Understanding what makes your partner who they are will help you navigate the difficult times in your relationship.

Conclusion

Cultivating compassion in your relationship can help you feel more connected to your partner and can help you navigate challenging times with greater ease. You can create a more

The Alchemy of Affection

compassionate and loving relationship by practicing active listening, empathy, forgiveness, gratitude, and offering support.

♥♥

Dr. Kevin Grold

Part III: The Gold of Love

CHAPTER 9: MINDFULNESS: THE ART OF LOVING ATTENTION

In a world full of distractions and demands, it can be challenging to be fully present in a relationship. This chapter explores the benefits of mindfulness for cultivating loving attention and fostering deeper connections with others. It covers the basics of a mindfulness practice, including breath awareness, what is called "body scanning," and mindful listening, and shows how these techniques can enhance intimacy and communication in relationships. It also addresses some challenges of practicing mindfulness in a relationship, such as dealing with conflict and navigating differences in values and priorities.

One of the most powerful ways to deepen your emotional connection with your partner is to **cultivate a sense of mindfulness** and presence in your relationship. When fully present with (or aware of) your partner, you can tune in to your partner's needs, desires, and emotions to foster intimacy and understanding.

Mindfulness means being engaged in the moment without judgment or distraction. It involves tuning in to your thoughts, feelings, and physical sensations. By cultivating mindfulness in your relationship, you can experience your partner with greater empathy, understanding, and compassion.

Practical Exercises for Cultivating Mindfulness and Presence in Your Relationship

Practice Mindful Breathing: One of the simplest and most effective ways to cultivate mindfulness is to focus on your breath. Sit in a comfortable position with your eyes closed. Take a few deep breaths and concentrate your attention on your breath. Notice the sensation of the air moving in and out of your nostrils, the rise and fall of your chest, and any other sensations in your body. When your mind wanders, gently bring your focus back to your breath. Take a few moments each day to sit quietly and focus on your breath. When you feel distracted or overwhelmed, take deep breaths to center yourself and return to the present moment. If you do this alone, you can present a better-centered person to your partner. If you do this together, then all the better!

Practice Loving Kindness Meditation: Loving-kindness meditation involves directing feelings of compassion and kindness toward yourself and others. Practice loving-kindness meditation by sending love and positive energy toward yourself and your partner. Repeat the following phrases silently to yourself: "May I be happy, may I be healthy, may I be loved, may I be at peace. May my partner be happy, may my partner be healthy, may my partner be loved, may my partner be at peace." Take a few moments each day to practice this meditation, focusing on sending love and positive energy toward your partner. This can help cultivate a sense of connection and understanding in your relationship.

Practice Mindful Listening: Set aside time to practice mindful listening with your partner. Take turns speaking and listening and focus on being fully present and engaged with each other. Mindful listening involves giving your full attention to your partner when they are talking, without judgment or distraction. When your partner is speaking, try to focus on their words and tune in to their tone of voice and body language. Resist the urge to interrupt or prepare your response; listen with an open mind and heart.

_____

Talk with the Bear

Choose a funny symbol for communication, such as a stuffed bear. Only the person holding the animal can speak, and then it is transferred to the other person only when you are done.

_____

Practice Mindful Touch: Physical touch is an important aspect of emotional connection, but it is often done mindlessly or without intention. When you touch your partner, try to do so with mindfulness and purpose, focusing on the sensation of their skin and the energy between you. This can help deepen your emotional connection and foster a sense of intimacy.

Examples of a Couple Using These Tips

Omar and Hamza

Omar and Hamza had been together for several years but

struggled because of a lack of an emotional connection. They were busy with work and other commitments and often felt like they were living separate lives. They decided to try cultivating mindfulness and presence in their relationship by practicing mindful breathing and loving-kindness meditation together. They also practiced mindful listening and touch, focusing on being fully present with each other. Over time, they noticed a more profound sense of connection and understanding in their relationship, and they felt more in tune with each other's needs and desires.

List of Exercises to Mindfully Improve Your Relationship

Start with yourself: Begin your mindfulness practice by focusing on your breathing. This will help you become more aware of your own reactions and feelings, which will help you be more present and attentive to your partner.

Create a mindfulness ritual: Set aside a specific time each day to practice mindfulness together. This could be a few minutes before bed, a morning meditation, or a regular nature walk.

Listen with your whole body: Pay attention to your partner's words, tone of voice, and body language. Try to tune out distractions and focus on what they are saying.

Use non-verbal cues: Use non-verbal cues to show your partner you are fully present and attentive. Maintain eye contact, nod your head, or touch their hand to show you are listening and engaged.

Practice empathy: Try to see things from your significant other's perspective. This will help you understand their needs and feelings and will make it easier for you to respond with love and compassion.

Avoid judgment: Avoid judging your partner's words or actions, even if they disagree with your opinions or beliefs. Instead, focus on understanding and accepting their point of view.

Examples

Kara and Madison

Kara and Madison had been married for ten years, but lately, they had felt disconnected and distant. They decided to try practicing mindfulness together and soon noticed a significant difference in their relationship. They began to listen to each other more deeply and communicate with more empathy and understanding. They also started expressing gratitude for each other regularly, which helped them feel more appreciated and loved.

Chandler and Laura

Chandler and Laura had always struggled with communication in their relationship. They decided to try practicing mindful listening together and found that it helped them connect on a deeper level. They could express their needs and feelings more clearly and better understand and support each other.

Practicing mindfulness can improve communication, empathy, understanding, and relationships. Mindful listening increases feelings of connection and intimacy between partners, and expressing gratitude promotes greater relationship satisfaction and happiness.

Remember, mindfulness is a skill, so do not worry if it does not come naturally to you at first. The more you practice, the easier it will become to be present in your relationship and give your partner the loving attention they deserve.

As you continue to practice mindfulness in your relationship, remember it is not about being perfect or getting everything right. Instead, it is about being open to the present moment and cultivating a sense of curiosity and non-judgment.

Here are additional tips for incorporating mindfulness into your relationship:

Schedule regular date nights: Make it a priority to have a regular date night, whether it's weekly or bi-weekly. Use this time to do something fun and engaging together, such as going out for dinner, seeing a movie, or walking in the park.

Take a weekend getaway: Plan a getaway to a place you both love and have always wanted to visit. This can be a great opportunity to escape the stress and demands of daily life and focus on each other.

Share activities and hobbies: Find common interests or activities you enjoy and make time to do them together. For example, cooking a meal together, hiking, or taking a dance class.

Create traditions: Establish rituals you both enjoy and look forward to. This can be as simple as having breakfast together every Sunday morning or watching a movie or your favorite series together on Friday nights.

Take a break from technology: In today's world, it can be easy to get distracted and lose sight of what is happening in the present moment. Try taking a break from your phone or computer. Set aside time to unplug from technology and focus on each other. Turn off your phones and engage in meaningful conversation, play games, or do something creative together.

Ultimately, the key to prioritizing mindfulness is to be intentional and consistent. Make it a priority to spend time together, communicate openly and honestly, and enjoy each other's company. By doing so, you can strengthen your relationship and deepen your connection with each other.

Change your Words, Change your Thinking, Change your Life Technology™

Instead of asking the generic, "How are you doing?" It would be more effective to ask, "Can we set aside a few minutes to connect with each other and talk about your day?" This will enable your partner to be ready and in the best frame of mind when you are both ready to connect.

♥♥

CHAPTER 10: GRATITUDE: CULTIVATING APPRECIATION

Gratitude is one of the most transformative emotions we can experience in relationships. Gratitude is the feeling of thankfulness and appreciation for the good things in our lives, including our loved ones. When we cultivate gratitude in our relationships, we can experience more joy, love, and connection.

Research has shown that practicing gratitude can positively impact our relationships. Couples who expressed gratitude toward each other experienced more relationship satisfaction and a deeper connection than those who did not express gratitude. Additionally, practicing gratitude increases feelings of happiness and well-being.

Here are a few ways in which this works:

Enhancing Positive Emotions: Cultivating joy and appreciation will help increase positive emotions within the relationship. Joy, love, and gratitude can help build intimacy, trust, and a sense of connection between partners. When partners experience positive emotions, they are more likely to feel closer and more loving toward one another.

Improving Communication: When couples cultivate joy and appreciation, they communicate more positively with one another. They are more likely to express their gratitude for one another and to share their positive feelings openly. This can help improve communication between partners and create a more loving and supportive atmosphere.

Reducing Negative Emotions: Cultivating joy and appreciation can also help reduce negative emotions within the relationship. When partners focus on the positive aspects of their relationship and express their gratitude for one another, they are less likely to feel resentful or critical. This can reduce conflict and create a more positive and loving atmosphere within the relationship.

The Grass is Always Greener Syndrome: No relationship is perfect, and every partner has flaws. Couples can learn to accept each other's imperfections and work together to overcome the extra challenges. Avoid comparing your relationship with others'. Every relationship is unique and comparing it with others will cause unnecessary stress and strain. Be happy for all the good your relationship provides.

Strengthening Resilience: Cultivating joy and appreciation can also help couples build resilience in facing challenges. When partners have a positive outlook on their relationship and can focus on the positive aspects of their partnership, they are better equipped to handle stress and challenging times. This can help strengthen the bond between partners and create a more loving and supportive union.

Practical Tips for Cultivating Gratitude in Your Relationship

Express gratitude daily: Take the time each day to express gratitude toward your partner. It can be as simple as saying "thank you" for something they did or expressing appreciation for who they are.

Keep a gratitude journal: Write down things you are grateful for daily in your relationship. This can help you focus on the positive aspects of your bond and increase your overall sense of gratitude.

Practice mindfulness: Be present and fully engage in the moments you spend with your partner. Notice the small things you appreciate about them and let them know.

Celebrate milestones: Celebrate milestones in your relationship, such as anniversaries, by expressing gratitude and appreciation for your journey together.

Create gratitude rituals: Create rituals in your relationship that focus on gratitude, such as sharing what you are grateful for during mealtimes or before bed.

Examples of Couples Who Have Successfully Cultivated Gratitude in Their Relationships

Rachel and Lily

Rachel and Lily started a gratitude journal, where they wrote down three things they were grateful for each day. They made a point to express their appreciation to each other regularly for both big and small gestures. This helped them stay attuned to the positive aspects of their relationship and each other's strengths.

An Exercise To Help You Cultivate Gratitude In Your Relationship

Gratitude Jar: Get a jar and some small pieces of paper. Daily, write down something you are grateful for in your relationship on paper and put it in the jar. This can be as simple as "I'm grateful for the way you make me coffee in the morning" or "I'm grateful for the way you always listen to me." Over time, the jar will fill up with notes of gratitude, and on days when one or both partners are feeling down, you can pull out a message and be reminded of all the significant times in your relationship. At the end of the month, if there are remaining notes in the jar, take the opportunity to read them together and commemorate the aspects of your relationship that you are grateful for. Embrace this moment as a chance to celebrate and appreciate the positives in your partnership.

Giving and Receiving Gifts

For some people, receiving gifts is a primary way of feeling loved and valued in a relationship. They appreciate the thought and effort of selecting and presenting a gift, regardless of its monetary value.

Examples Of How Gifts Can Be A Way To Communicate Love

Meaningful gifts: Giving a gift that is personal and meaningful can make someone feel deeply loved and understood. For example, give someone a book by their favorite author or a piece of jewelry that has sentimental value.

Unexpected surprises: Surprising someone with a thoughtful gift can make them feel special and loved. For example, leaving a small gift or a note of appreciation on their pillow before they wake up or having a bouquet of flowers delivered to their office.

Celebrations: Giving gifts to celebrate special occasions such as birthdays, anniversaries, or holidays can be a way to show love and appreciation — for example, planning a surprise birthday party or offering a heartfelt gift on Valentine's Day.

Thoughtful gestures: Small gestures can also be meaningful gifts for someone who values receiving gifts. For example, bringing home their favorite snack after a long day at work or surprising them with coffee or tea in the morning.

An Example of a Couple Cultivating Joy and Appreciation in Their Relationship

Amy and Jake

Amy and Jake have been married for five years, and they consciously try to cultivate joy and appreciation in their relationship. They have a weekly date night where they try new restaurants or activities, and they make it a point to express their gratitude for each other regularly.

One day, as Amy was doing the dishes, Jake approached her and hugged her. "I just want you to know how much I appreciate you," he said. "You always make our home feel so warm and inviting, and I'm grateful for everything you do."

Amy turned around and smiled at Jake. "Thank you for saying that; it means a lot to me," she said. "And I appreciate you too. You always make me laugh and feel loved."

Later that week, they went on their weekly date night and tried a new sushi restaurant. As they returned to their car, Amy turned to Jake and said, "I had so much fun tonight. Thank you for always planning these fun date nights for us."

Jake grinned. "Of course, anything to make you happy," he said.

Amy and Jake strengthen their bond by cultivating joy and appreciation in their relationship and creating a positive, loving environment for their marriage.

Change your Words, Change your Thinking, Change your Life Technology™

Telling your friends that you are grateful for your partner will help your friends to support your relationship. The comments will also be repeated to your mate at some point and give you even more fun *love points*.

In an earlier part of this book, we discussed hurtful words that can be hard to take back. Now let us look at the positive statements you can say to your partner. Unfortunately, for some reason, you can say ten positive things and one negative statement, and everyone will remember the negative statement. So, work on keeping the ratio of positive statements high!

Dr. Kevin Grold

Positive Statements That Couples Can Say to Each Other

- I love you more every day
- I'm so grateful to have you in my life
- You're amazing just the way you are
- I appreciate everything you do for me
- I admire your strength and resilience
- You make me feel so happy and fulfilled
- I trust you completely
- I'm proud to be with you
- You're my best friend
- I respect and value you
- I'm so lucky to have found you
- You inspire me to be a better person
- I love spending time with you
- You're the most important person in my life
- I believe in you and your dreams
- You always make me laugh and smile
- I feel safe and supported when I'm with you

- You're a great partner and teammate
- I'm committed to making this relationship work
- You bring so much joy to my life

See if you feel any of the above statements feel right to you. If so, express that statement to your partner. Also consider making your own. Be creative! By practicing positive communication and affirmations, you can strengthen the bond between you and your partner.

Conclusion

Practicing gratitude can have a profound impact on your relationship. By intentionally cultivating gratitude, you can transform how you perceive your partner, connection, and life together. Engaging in daily gratitude practices, such as keeping a journal or creating gratitude rituals, can help you to deepen your connection with your partner and experience more joy and appreciation in your relationship. By focusing on the positive aspects of your partnership and expressing gratitude for one another, you can enhance positive emotions, improve communication, reduce negative emotions, and build resilience in the face of challenges. So why not try incorporating some gratitude practices into your daily life and see how they can enhance your relationship?

♥♥

CHAPTER 11: SERVICE: EXPRESSING LOVE THROUGH ACTION

Love is not just an emotion we feel toward someone; it is also an action we can express through service and kindness. When we love someone, we want to show them we care and are there for them. This chapter explores the importance of service in relationships and provides practical tips and exercises to help you express your love through action and kindness.

The Power of Service in Relationships

Service is an act of kindness that we do for others without expecting anything in return. It is a selfless act that shows our love and care for others. When we serve our partners, we portray our love and appreciation for them and create a bond of trust and intimacy.

Couples who engage in acts of service toward each other have a stronger relationship and are more satisfied with their relationship than couples who do not. This is because service acts help build trust, intimacy, and a sense of security in the relationship.

Practical Tips for Expressing Love through Service

Make a list of your partner's needs

The first step in expressing love through service is to find out what your partner needs. This could be as simple as making them breakfast in bed or helping them with their workload. Ask your partner what they need and how you can help. Often, we assume we know what our partner wants or needs. Take some time to sit down and list what your partner needs from you – it could be as simple as help with the dishes or as complex as emotional support during a difficult time. Use this list as a guide for ways you can offer your service to your partner. Be sure your partner is helping with this list (and hopefully, they want to make a list for you as well).

Do Things Without Being Asked

Sometimes, the best way to show love is to do things without being asked. This could be as simple as doing the dishes or taking out the trash. When you do this, you show your partner that you care and are willing to go the extra mile for them.

_____

IMPORTANT: You may be doing things for your partner and feeling like you are a remarkable, loving person because you are doing exactly what YOU want to experience. This is a very common mistake. DO NOT assume that what makes you feel loved is what makes your partner feel loved. Be sure to ask!

_____

Pay Attention to the Little Things

Small acts of service can go a long way in showing your love and appreciation for your partner. This could be as simple as leaving a love note in their lunchbox or bringing them a cup of tea when working late. Pay attention to the little things your partner likes and try to incorporate them into your service.

Be Consistent

Consistency is vital when it comes to expressing love through service. Make it a habit to do things for your partner regularly, even small things. This will help to create a sense of security and trust in your relationship.

Examples of Couples Using Service to Express Love

Jo Jo and Eko

Jo Jo and Eko have been together for ten years. Jo Jo works long hours as a nurse, and Eko is a stay-at-home dad. Despite their busy schedules, they make time for each other and always find ways to express their love through service. Eko often makes dinner for Jo Jo after a long day at work, and she helps Eko with the kids when he needs a break.

Exercise

The Kindness Challenge

For this exercise, each partner commits to performing one small act of kindness for their partner every day for a week. These acts of service can be anything from making them breakfast in bed to leaving them a thoughtful note and is best when tailored to your partner's individual needs and preferences.

Exercises to Improve Your Relationship Through Service

Make a List of Things Your Partner Likes

List things your partner likes and try to incorporate them into your acts of service. This could be something as simple as making them their favorite meal or buying them a small gift. Ask your mate if they like the list and feel it is complete. When you show your partner that you pay attention to what they like, you show them that you care about their happiness.

Here are some additional practical tips and exercises for couples to express love through action and kindness:

Date Night: Schedule regular date nights where you and your partner take turns planning an activity or outing that you both enjoy. This shows that you value your partner's interests and are willing to put in the effort to make them happy.

Surprise Chores: Take on tasks or chores your partner dislikes or finds challenging. For example, if your partner hates doing the laundry, offer to take on that responsibility for a while. This shows that you care about his or her well-being and helps to alleviate stress and build teamwork in your relationship.

Shared Service: Find ways to serve together in your community or volunteer for a cause you care about. This enables you to give back, make a positive impact, and strengthen your bond as a couple by working toward a shared goal. Volunteering together can be a powerful way to connect and give back to your community. Find a cause you both care about and dedicate some time to serving others.

Surprise your partner: Doing something unexpected for your partner can be an excellent way to show your love and appreciation. Whether it is running a bath for them after a long day, or doing a chore they have been putting off, the element of surprise can make your act of service even more meaningful.

Show up for your partner: Being present and attentive when your partner needs you can be a powerful way to demonstrate your love. This could mean going with them to a doctor's appointment, staying up late to talk through a problem, or simply listening when they need to vent.

Take turns serving: A healthy relationship is reciprocal, and it is vital for both partners to give and receive. Take turns offering your service to each other and be open to accepting help when needed.

Here are 20 acts of service ideas that couples can do for each other:

1. Cook a special meal for your partner
2. Do the grocery shopping for the week
3. Clean the house or apartment
4. Do the laundry
5. Wash the dishes
6. Take care of the kids to give your partner some alone time
7. Bring your partner breakfast in bed
8. Take care of the pets
9. Offer to run errands for your partner
10. Give your partner a massage
11. Fill up their car with gas
12. Plan a surprise date night

13. Offer to help your partner with a project or task they've been putting off
14. Bring your partner a cup of tea or coffee while they work
15. Take care of your partner when they are sick
16. Help your partner organize their closet or dresser
17. Offer to help your partner pack for a trip
18. Get up early to make breakfast for your partner before work
19. Make a special treat for your partner, like homemade cookies or cake
20. Offer to drive your partner to their appointments or meetings

PRO TIP

It is easy to get caught up in our busy lives and forget to make time for our partner's needs. Set aside regular time to focus on serving your partner, whether on a weekly date night or a daily check-in, to see how you can be of service to your partner and your relationship.

Change your Words, Change your Thinking, Change your Life Technology™

Instead of doing what YOU would like and saying, "Here, I did this for you." Try saying, "You have a lot going on right now; I would like to help; how can I best be of service?" This will let your partner know you are trying, and they can provide guidance as to the most helpful type of service.

At the end of the week, take some time to reflect on how these small acts of kindness have impacted your relationship. Did you feel more connected to your person? Did you notice an improvement in their mood or well-being? How did it feel to give and receive these acts of kindness?

Conclusion

By consciously expressing love through action and kindness, you can strengthen the bond between you and your partner and create a happier, more fulfilling relationship.

Service is not about keeping score or trying to outdo your partner. It is about showing love and care through actions and finding joy in making your partner's life a little easier and more fulfilling. By practicing the gift of service in your relationship, you can build a strong foundation of love and support that will stand the test of time.

Part IV: The Everlasting Bond of Love

CHAPTER 12: PASSION: CULTIVATING A SEXUAL BOND

Maintaining sexual intimacy in a long-term relationship can be challenging. However, it's crucial to understand that sex is not just about physical pleasure; it also fosters emotional and psychological intimacy between partners. Sexual intimacy can strengthen the bond between partners and enhance their overall relationship satisfaction. Therefore, it is important that couples prioritize and invest in their sexual connection to maintain a strong and healthy relationship.

To enhance sexual intimacy, it is vital to learn about your partner's erogenous zones, explore each other's bodies, and engage in foreplay. These activities can help build sexual tension and arousal, leading to a more satisfying sexual experience. Moreover, maintaining physical health through exercise, healthy eating, and adequate sleep can improve sexual function and energy.

PRO TIP

Sex usually begins as a mutually enjoyable experience for both partners. It can also transform into what one partner feels is a chore or be seen as a gift grudgingly given from one partner to the other. Pay attention to your partner's body language and verbal cues during sexual intimacy. If your partner seems disinterested, distant, or unengaged, it may be a sign that underlying issues need to be addressed. Similarly, if you or your partner regularly avoids or rejects sexual intimacy, it could be a sign of deeper relationship issues. Communication is key in addressing these issues and finding ways to improve your sexual experiences together.

Have an open conversation with your partner: Open and honest communication around sexual desires, boundaries, and needs is crucial in building a strong and healthy sexual connection. Discuss what you enjoy and do not enjoy and encourage your significant other to do the same. Discussing your desires, boundaries, and needs with your partner can help improve your sexual experiences and increase feelings of intimacy. Do not be afraid to talk about what you like and do not like, and then be open to listening to the same from your partner. It is important to feel comfortable when discussing desires and preferences and actively listen to and respect each other's boundaries and needs.

Talking About Sex

Setting the tone: Before talking about sexual needs and desires, couples need to create a safe and comfortable space where they can have an open and honest conversation. This might involve setting aside dedicated time to talk, choosing a private and relaxing environment, and ensuring both partners feel comfortable and respected.

Expressing desires: One partner might desire to try a new sexual position or experiment with a specific kink or fetish. The other partner listens actively and without judgment and be open to exploring the possibility.

Asking for feedback: Couples can also ask for feedback on their sexual performance and offer suggestions for improving both partners' experiences. This can involve discussing what each person likes and dislikes and exploring different ways to achieve mutual satisfaction.

Addressing concerns: Discuss any concerns or fears around sex, such as performance anxiety or issues related to body image. This can help to build trust and deepen intimacy in the relationship.

Sharing fantasies: Couples can also discuss their sexual fantasies and explore the possibility of fulfilling them together. This can be a way to add novelty and excitement to the relationship and deepen the level of intimacy between partners.

Respecting boundaries: Couples must respect each other's boundaries and only engage in sexual activities that both individuals are comfortable with. It is important that couples discuss and agree on boundaries before engaging in new sexual experiences.

Overall, open and honest communication about sexual needs and desires can help couples to deepen their connection and enhance their relationship in a positive and fulfilling way.

An Example of Lucy and Jah Having a Conversation About Trying New Things Sexually

Jah: "Lucy, I've been thinking about us trying something new in the bedroom. I've been reading about some new techniques and positions that could be exciting for us. Are you open to exploring that with me?"

Lucy: "I'm definitely open to trying new things with you, Jah. What were you thinking?"

Jah: "I thought we could try some more adventurous positions, like the reverse cowgirl or the wheelbarrow. And maybe we could try incorporating some toys or role-playing too."

Lucy: "Wow, that does sound adventurous! I'm open to trying those positions, and I'm also curious about toys and role-playing. Let's talk more about it and figure out what we're both comfortable with."

Jah: "Absolutely, let's take it slow and make sure we're both comfortable with everything. I'm excited to explore this new aspect of our relationship with you."

PRO TIP

Be mindful that comments about your partner's appearance or actions can sometimes trigger underlying self-esteem issues. Your partner may misinterpret your remarks, leading to hurt feelings or misunderstandings. To avoid this, it's best to express your thoughts and feelings positively and be supportive. Focus on highlighting your partner's strengths and qualities you admire. This approach can help build their self-esteem and create a more positive and uplifting environment in your relationship.

Safe Space Sex Growth Communication

Create a safe and supportive environment with your partner where you will have open conversations about sex. Establish an agreement to listen to each other without judgment and provide encouragement. Recognize that discussing uncomfortable topics can strengthen your bond and deepen your relationship, particularly when met with positive and supportive responses. Start by writing down sexual questions or desires you feel are challenging to share. Additionally, include answers to all the conversation starters provided below. Assign numbers to the questions based on the difficulty level in communicating with your partner. Begin with the easiest question and share it with your partner, observing their response. Encourage your partner to do the same. If both of you feel comfortable, progress through the list. If discomfort arises, openly discuss your feelings and explore ways to facilitate a more comfortable sharing environment and save the remainder of the questions for a future time.

Dr. Kevin Grold

Some starters for your sex discussion

- One thing I find particularly exciting is:
- Sexually, I am a bit hesitant to bring up:
- I would like more of:
- I would like to try:
- I am worried you might be turned off if I:
- I would like not to do this:
- Some words, sounds, or phrases that really turn me on:
- It feels really good when you:
- A fantasy or role-play scenario I have always wanted to try is:
- We could be exploring this sexual issue further:

Creating a safe and non-judgmental environment is crucial for these discussions. Take your time, be understanding, and be open to each other's desires and boundaries.

*** *** ***

Explore your sexuality

One of the best ways to improve your sexual relationship is to explore your sexuality. This involves understanding your desires and needs and expressing them to your partner. Take the time to learn about your body and what feels good. Masturbation can be a helpful tool for exploring your sexuality and learning what feels good. Take some time to think about what you want in the bedroom and what you would like to try.

Experiment

Sexual boredom can be a problem in long-term relationships. To keep things interesting, try experimenting with new things in the bedroom. This can involve trying new positions, using sex toys, or even role-playing. Be open-minded and willing to try new things, but also respect your boundaries and your partner's.

Role-play

Couples can use fantasy to role-play, taking on different personas and exploring different scenarios. This can help spice up their sex life and bring excitement and novelty to the relationship.

Daydreaming

Daydreaming is another way couples can use fantasy to improve their relationships. They can imagine romantic or exciting scenarios, such as going on a dream vacation together or achieving a shared goal. This can help build anticipation and excitement in the relationship.

Practice Mindfulness

Mindfulness can help you to be fully present during sexual activity, which can enhance your enjoyment and deepen your connection with your partner. Focus on your breath, your body, and the sensations you are experiencing. Avoid distractions and be fully present in the moment. This can help you and your partner feel more connected and increase feelings of pleasure.

Practice Sexual Gratitude

Expressing gratitude can also improve your sexual relationship. Take the time to appreciate your partner and the things they do for you. Compliment them on their physical appearance, performance in the bedroom, and efforts to strengthen your relationship. Expressing gratitude can help build a stronger emotional connection and create a positive feedback loop, leading to greater sexual satisfaction.

Schedule Intimacy

One key to maintaining sexual fulfillment is prioritizing it regularly by setting aside specific times, just like scheduling a date night. This helps build anticipation and excitement around sexual intimacy.

Take care of your physical health

Taking care of your physical health can also improve your sexual relationship. Exercise regularly, eat a healthy diet, and get enough sleep. This can improve your energy levels, mood, and well-being. Additionally, certain physical conditions can affect sexual function, so speak with your doctor if you are experiencing any issues.

*** *** ***

Steps You Can Follow to Give a Sensual Massage

Set the Mood: Create a relaxing, romantic atmosphere before you begin the massage. Dim the lights, light candles, and play soft music to set the mood.

Use High-Quality Oils: Use high-quality massage oils or lotions designed explicitly for sensual massages. You can use scented oils for a more sensual experience.

Relax Your Own Mind and Body: By being relaxed yourself, you can pass that relaxing energy to your partner and better tune into their responses, likes, and dislikes. Try not to be in a tense, rushed state.

Start with a Warm-Up: Start the massage with a warm-up. Use gentle, long strokes to warm and relax your partner's muscles.

Use Varied Strokes: Use a combination of different strokes to create a variety of sensations. Use gentle, circular motions to relax the muscles and firmer strokes for a deeper massage.

Focus on Erogenous Zones: Focus on your partner's erogenous zones, such as the neck, back, shoulders, and feet. These areas are particularly sensitive and can be very pleasurable when massaged.

Pay Attention to Breathing: Pay attention to your partner's breathing. Encourage them to breathe deeply and slowly and use your own breathing to create a rhythm and connection between you.

Use Your Hands and Body: Use your hands, fingers, and forearms to create different sensations, and use your body weight to add pressure and depth to the massage.

Communicate with Your Partner: Communicate with your partner throughout the massage. Ask them what feels good and what they want more of. Also, do your best to read the non-verbal signs coming from your partner regarding what feels good and what to avoid.

End with a Cool-Down: End the massage with a cool-down. Use gentle strokes and light pressure to help your partner relax and return slowly to a normal alert state.

Remember, a sensual massage is about creating a loving, intimate connection with your partner. Take your time, be patient, and focus on creating a positive, loving atmosphere for the massage.

*** *** ***

PRO TIP

Do not squirt the oil directly onto your partner's body. It can be cold and shocking. Warm the massage oil between your hands and then apply it to your mate.

*** *** ***

Dr. Kevin Grold

Kegel Exercises

Kegel exercises, also known as pelvic floor exercises, involve contracting and relaxing the pelvic floor muscles. These exercises can be beneficial for men and women in improving sexual function and intimacy. Research has shown that performing Kegel exercises can increase the strength and endurance of the pelvic floor muscles, leading to improved sexual function and more intense orgasms. For women, stronger pelvic floor muscles can improve vaginal tone, which can enhance sexual sensations and improve orgasmic response. For men, stronger pelvic floor muscles can improve erectile function and control, leading to longer-lasting and more satisfying sexual experiences.

Here are detailed instructions on how to perform Kegel exercises

Identify the pelvic floor muscles: The first step is to locate the muscles you need to work on. The easiest way to do this is by stopping the flow of urine midstream. The muscles you use to do this are your pelvic floor muscles.

Empty your bladder: After identifying your pelvic floor muscles, empty your bladder before starting the exercises.

Contract the pelvic floor muscles: Tighten your pelvic floor muscles by squeezing them as hard as possible. Hold the contraction for 5-10 seconds, then release.

Relax the muscles: Relax your pelvic floor muscles and rest for 5-10 seconds before starting the next contraction.

Repeat the exercise: Repeat steps 3-4 for a total of 10-15 repetitions.

Increase the duration of the contraction: As you become more comfortable with the exercise, gradually increase the time of the contraction to 10 seconds or more.

Don't hold your breath: It's important to breathe normally during the exercise and not hold your breath.

Don't squeeze other muscles: Ensure you only contract your pelvic floor muscles, not your buttocks, thighs, or abdomen.

Do the exercises regularly: Aim to do Kegel exercises at least three times a day. You can do them anytime, anywhere, as they are discreet and can be done while sitting, standing, or lying down.

Be patient: Like any other exercise, it may take some time before you start seeing the benefits of Kegels. It's essential to be consistent and patient with the practices to see the results.

Sexual Problems

Sexual problems can be a common issue that couples face, and they can cause stress and tension in the relationship. Here are the three most common sexual problems for couples, along with some potential solutions:

Low desire: One of the most common sexual problems is a lack of desire or interest in sex. Various factors, including stress, relationship problems, depression, medication side effects, and hormonal changes, can cause this. To address low desire, couples can try scheduling regular date nights or sexual intimacy time, engaging in activities that promote relaxation and stress reduction (such as yoga or meditation), and talking openly and honestly about their feelings and desires.

Erectile dysfunction: Erectile dysfunction (ED) is the inability to achieve or maintain an erection during sexual activity.

Physical or psychological factors like diabetes, stress, high blood pressure, anxiety, or depression can cause this. To address ED, couples can try practicing relaxation techniques (such as deep breathing or progressive muscle relaxation), seeking medical treatment (such as medication or therapy), and exploring different sexual positions or activities that don't rely solely on an erection.

Painful intercourse: Painful intercourse, also known as dyspareunia, is a common sexual problem that various factors, such as vaginal dryness (i.e., post-menopause, caused by estrogen loss), infections, or certain medical conditions, can cause. To address painful intercourse, couples can try using lubrication to reduce friction and discomfort, seeking medical treatment for any underlying conditions, trying different sexual positions or activities that are more comfortable, and practicing relaxation techniques to reduce anxiety and tension.

It's important to note that these solutions may not work for every individual, and seeking the help of a trained therapist or medical professional may be necessary in some cases. Additionally, couples need to communicate openly and honestly with each other about their sexual concerns and need to work together to find solutions that work for both partners.

Change your Words, Change your Thinking, Change your Life Technology™

Be careful how you talk to your partner about your sexual desires. Your partner may have self-esteem issues and be triggered if your ideas are not presented gently and encouragingly. Being positive and reinforcing toward your partner can build trust and comfort, allowing you to explore your sexuality further.

Differing Levels of Sexual Desire and Using Compromise

It is unreasonable to believe both partners will maintain equal sexual desire throughout a long-term, loving relationship. Therefore, this will be an issue at some point. Couples need skills to face this issue, so their love remains strong.

Compromise is an essential aspect of any healthy relationship, including in the area of sexual desire. When partners have different levels of sexual desire, finding a compromise that works for both partners can be challenging but crucial for maintaining a fulfilling and healthy relationship.

Compromise involves finding a middle ground that both partners can agree on. This may include negotiating and discussing specific sexual activities or the frequency of sexual activity. It is essential for both partners to be open and honest about their needs and desires and to listen to each other without judgment.

A key element of compromise is that it is a two-way street. Both individuals need to be willing to give and take to find a solution that works for both of them. This means being willing to make changes or try new things, even if they're outside of your comfort zone.

It's also important to recognize that compromise may be challenging and require some sacrifice from both partners. However, if both partners are committed to finding a solution, compromise can help strengthen the relationship and create a more profound sense of trust and intimacy.

When finding a compromise around sexual desire, it's important to remember that there is no one-size-fits-all solution. Every couple is unique, and what works for one couple may not work for another. The key is approaching the issue with an open mind, a willingness to listen and communicate, and a commitment to finding a solution that works for both partners.

Conclusion

Cultivating and sustaining sexual energy and fulfillment in a loving relationship requires intentional effort and investment. Prioritizing sexual intimacy, communicating openly and honestly, and exploring new experiences together can help couples tap into the transformative power of sexual energy and build on their lasting, passionate relationship.

CHAPTER 13: MAINTAINING INTIMACY IN A LOVING RELATIONSHIP

Maintaining intimacy in a romantic relationship is essential for building and sustaining a solid emotional connection between partners. While sexual intimacy (discussed in chapter 12) is one way to strengthen that connection, there are other ways to maintain intimacy in a relationship that can be just as important.

This chapter will explore intimacy in detail and look at the most effective ways to keep your relationship strong and loving.

Types of Intimacy

Emotional intimacy: Emotional intimacy is about sharing with your partner and allowing yourself to be vulnerable. This type of intimacy is built through deep conversations, sharing your feelings and thoughts, and actively listening to your partner's experiences. Couples can strengthen emotional intimacy by setting aside time each day to check in with each other and share how they're feeling.

Intellectual intimacy: Intellectual intimacy involves sharing ideas, thoughts, and interests with your significant other. Couples can maintain intellectual intimacy by engaging in activities that challenge their minds, such as taking a class or discussing current events.

Spiritual intimacy: Spiritual intimacy is about sharing a sense of purpose or meaning with your partner. This can involve attending religious services or engaging in spiritual practices such as meditation or prayer.

Physical Intimacy: Physical intimacy doesn't always have to be sexual. Couples can maintain physical intimacy by engaging in activities that promote touch and closeness, such as holding hands, cuddling, or giving massages. Physical intimacy is an essential part of any romantic relationship. It helps to strengthen the emotional bond between partners and promotes feelings of closeness and connection.

Exercises to Maintain Intimacy

Share a meaningful memory: Share a memory you cherish and discuss how it felt.

Write love letters: Write a heartfelt letter to your partner expressing your love and appreciation for them. You can commit to writing love letters to each other regularly.

Take turns asking deep questions: Ask each other thought-provoking questions such as "What do you want to accomplish in the next year?" or "What was a turning point in your life?"

Ten More Deep And Thought-Provoking Questions You Can Use to Learn More About Each Other and Create Deeper Intimacy

1. What is one thing you're most proud of and why?
2. If you could change one decision you made in your past, what would it be and why?
3. What is your greatest fear, and how has it impacted your life?
4. What do you think is the meaning of life?
5. What are your biggest regrets, and how have they influenced who you are today?
6. If you could relive one day of your life, what day would it be, and what would you do differently?

7. What are your dreams and aspirations for the future, and how can I help support you in achieving them?
8. What is one thing you wish your partner knew about you that they don't?
9. If you could ask me one question you've hesitated to ask, what would it be?
10. What are your core values, and how do you try to live by them in your daily life?

These questions can help you explore each other's beliefs, values, fears, and hopes, leading to a deeper understanding and connection. It is essential to approach these questions with an open mind and heart, ready to listen and share without judgment or criticism.

Romance

For this task, keep in mind that you are trying to do what your partner wants, not what you would like. Consider what makes your partner feel loved as you read this list.

Dr. Kevin Grold

Romantic Gestures to Show Your Love And Affection

- Write a love letter or send a romantic text message
- Prepare a surprise dinner or breakfast in bed for your partner
- Create a scrapbook or photo album of your memories together
- Buy your partner flowers or their favorite treats
- Plan a surprise weekend getaway or staycation
- Dress up in a sexy outfit and surprise your partner in some unusual way
- Prepare a relaxing bath with candles and soft music for your partner
- Give your partner a massage or book a couple's spa day
- Watch a romantic movie together and snuggle up
- Leave little love notes around the house or in your partner's belongings
- Take a romantic walk or hike together

- Plan a surprise picnic in a scenic location
- Create a playlist of songs that are meaningful to your relationship
- Make a homemade gift, such as a painting or jewelry
- Write a poem or a song for your partner
- Take a dance class or learn a new hobby together

Remember, the most important thing is to do what feels authentic and meaningful to your relationship. By showing your partner love and affection through romantic gestures, you can strengthen your connection and deepen your emotional bond.

Change your Words, Change your Thinking, Change your Life Technology™

Deepen Intimacy by making your words sacred: Instead of saying to your partner, "Love Ya'" why not agree to say "I love you" only to your committed partner and save "Love Ya" for family and friends? This makes your statement more meaningful.

Understand Your Love Language

People can feel loved in many different ways, and if you want to be deeply intimate with your partner, it is essential to recognize and understand the various ways in which your partner feels loved. Some of the most common ways people feel loved include:

Words of Affirmation: People who feel loved through words of affirmation value verbal expressions of love, such as compliments, praise, and affectionate statements. Hearing that they are appreciated, loved, and valued can make a big difference in their emotional well-being.

Quality Time: For some people, spending quality time together is the most important way to feel loved. This means undivided attention and dedicated time for activities, conversations, or simply being together.

Acts of Service: People who feel loved through acts of service value gestures of kindness and support, such as cooking a meal, doing the laundry, or running errands. These actions can demonstrate love and care in a tangible and meaningful way.

Physical Touch: Physical touch is a powerful way to show affection and love, whether through hugging, kissing, holding hands, or other forms of physical intimacy. People who feel loved through physical touch often feel more connected and secure with their partner.

Gifts: Some people feel loved by receiving gifts, whether a thoughtful, meaningful present or a simple gesture of appreciation. Gifts can show that someone has been thinking about them and that their partner cares about their happiness.

Understand your partner's love language and be aware of your own, so you can communicate love in a way that resonates most with them. This understanding can foster more intimacy in your relationship and help you build a stronger connection with your partner.

PRO TIP #1

Dr. Gary Chapman has written several excellent books discussing love languages. If you want more details, read one of his books about the five love languages.

PRO TIP #2

Do not assume that the way you feel love is the same as the way your partner feels love. Discuss this topic in detail with your partner; you might be surprised by what you learn.

Plan For Tough Times

Keep intimacy going by planning for future issues, such as jealousy and stress, before they happen.

Jealousy

Jealousy is common in many romantic relationships and can cause significant problems if not appropriately addressed.

Planning can help couples deal with jealousy more effectively. Here are some suggestions.

Acknowledge the issue: The first step in dealing with jealousy is recognizing it exists. Couples ought to openly discuss their jealousy and how it affects them individually and as a couple.

Identify triggers: Once the couple has acknowledged the issue, they can start to identify what triggers their feelings of jealousy. It could be situations, people, or behaviors that spark those emotions. By understanding what triggers jealousy, the couple can plan to avoid those triggers or prepare for them.

Communication: Good communication is essential for any

healthy relationship and is crucial when dealing with jealousy. Couples ought to agree to communicate openly and honestly about their feelings and work together to find solutions.

Set boundaries: Couples ought to set clear boundaries with which both partners feel comfortable. These boundaries can be about time spent with others, communication with ex-partners, or other behaviors that may lead to jealousy.

Security: Discuss what makes you feel more secure in difficult situations: You might tell your partner that sitting close and holding hands at parties makes you feel more connected and less jealous. Talk over what feels comforting for you in difficult situations.

Seek professional help: If the feelings of jealousy persist despite your efforts, then consider seeking the help of a professional counselor. A therapist can provide guidance on how to work through jealousy and strengthen the relationship for your particular circumstance.

Overall, planning to deal with jealousy in a relationship involves acknowledging the issue, identifying triggers, communicating openly, setting boundaries, planning activities together, and seeking professional help if necessary.

Stress

Stress will occur in your relationship, and it is healthy to discuss how best to assist your partner before things get overloaded.

Discuss stress triggers: The first step in planning to deal with stress in a relationship is identifying what triggers anxiety for each partner. For example, work-related stress, financial issues, family problems, or health concerns can all cause stress. Once the couple has identified their stress triggers, they can work together to develop a plan to manage them.

Create a stress management plan: The couple can develop a plan to manage stress together. This plan can include healthy coping mechanisms such as exercise, meditation, or hobbies the couple enjoys together. They can also discuss managing their stress levels, such as setting realistic expectations, delegating tasks, and prioritizing self-care.

Ask your partner: Discuss in advance by sitting your partner down and asking what you can do specifically when your partner is feeling stressed or having a bad day. Planning in advance will lead to more success in your relationship because in the moment, it is harder to find those things to help, but being prepared will keep that from being a problem. Mind reading, or assuming what your partner wants on a stressful day, will lead to problems.

Conclusion

Maintaining intimacy in a relationship is something you can accomplish by feeding and nurturing the sacred connection you both have. Following the suggestions in this chapter, you will see a more profound bond develop between you both.

CHAPTER 14: TRANSCENDENT LOVE: FINDING THE DIVINE IN YOUR PARTNERSHIP

Love is a powerful force that can transcend the ordinary and connect us with something greater than ourselves. Whether you believe in a higher power or not, there is something deeply spiritual about the experience of love. In this chapter, we will explore how to tap into the transcendent nature of love and deepen our connections with our partners.

It is important to remember that the idea of finding the divine in human relationships is a deeply personal one. Some couples may find that spirituality and religion play a significant role in their relationship, while others may not. Regardless, the key is approaching your relationship with a sense of reverence and awe, recognizing the beauty and power of love to connect us to something greater than ourselves.

Connect with the Divine

People who connect with something larger than themselves are generally happier and healthier. This connection can take many forms, including a sense of purpose, a feeling of community, or a spiritual practice. Regarding romantic relationships, feeling like you and your partner are part of something bigger than your individual selves can create a sense of awe, gratitude, and meaning that can deepen your bond.

One way to tap into this sense of transcendence is to practice gratitude. Gratitude is the practice of focusing on the positive things in your life and expressing appreciation for them. When you focus on what you are grateful for, you are more likely to feel connected to something larger than yourself. Take time each day to reflect on what you appreciate about your partner and relationship. Share your gratitude with your partner and encourage them to do the same.

Another way to tap into the transcendent nature of love is to practice mindfulness while experiencing and discussing the world more significant than your partnership. Mindfulness is being present and in tune to your surroundings and partner in the current moment. When fully present with your partner, you are more likely to feel connected and in tune with their needs and emotions.

Practical Transcendent Tips

Here are some simple ways to bring a larger feeling of purpose to your relationship.

Find a shared sense of purpose: Whether volunteering together, starting a project together, or pursuing a shared goal, finding a shared sense of purpose can create a sense of meaning and connection that can deepen your bond.

Practice spiritual mindfulness: Take time daily to be fully present with your partner. This can include activities like meditating, going for a walk, or simply sitting and talking without distractions.

Connect with nature: Spending time in nature can be a powerful way to feel connected to something larger than yourself. Consider going to a park or the beach, taking a hike, or going on a camping trip with your partner.

Connect with a higher power: Spending time in spiritual practice in whatever form is right for you. This can be a powerful way to connect to something larger than yourself.

Create a shared vision board: Sit down with your mate and create a vision board together. Include images and words that represent your shared goals and values. Display the vision board in a prominent place where you will both appreciate it.

Examples of Couples Using the Tips

Sofia and Thomas: Sofia and Thomas are both passionate about helping others. They started a nonprofit organization together that provides support to people in need. They have deepened their connection and created a sense of meaning in their relationship through their shared sense of purpose.

Rachel and Diego: Rachel and Diego practice mindfulness together each day. They take a few minutes to meditate together or sit and talk without distractions. This practice has helped them feel more present and connected.

Sacred Words

Adding sacred words to compliments can be a positive way to show love, respect, and appreciation. Sacred words are often associated with religious or spiritual contexts and can carry a deeper meaning for individuals and couples who value these beliefs. However, it is essential to approach this practice with sensitivity and respect for the beliefs and traditions of both partners.

When incorporating sacred words into compliments, it is crucial to ensure that both partners are comfortable with the chosen words and their meanings. It is essential to have open communication and respect each other's beliefs and preferences.

Some examples of sacred words that can be added to compliments for couples include:

- blessed
- graceful
- divine
- holy
- sacred
- godly
- spiritual
- anointed

Compliments that include sacred words can deepen the emotional connection between couples and create reverence and respect for each other. For example, a compliment like

"You are a divine being, and I feel so blessed to have you in my life" can express the speaker's admiration and appreciation while adding a spiritual or religious dimension to the relationship.

Ten Examples Of Compliments That Include Sacred Words

- You are a sensitive partner, and I am grateful for your love and support
- Your kindness is a blessing, bringing so much joy to my life
- You have a graceful spirit that inspires me to be a better person every day
- I feel so blessed to have you as my soulmate and share this sacred journey with you
- Your wisdom is holy, and I treasure every moment we spend together
- Your love is sacred to me, and I feel honored to be able to share it with you

- Your generosity is a divine gift, and it touches the lives of everyone around you
- I am in awe of your strength and resilience, which I see as a manifestation of the divine within you
- Your love is like a holy fire that burns brightly in my heart and strengthens me
- You are an anointed partner, and I am blessed to be able to call you mine

Conclusion

Ultimately, the transcendence of love is about recognizing that our relationships are more than just physical or emotional connections. They are opportunities to connect with something larger than us and to experience the divine in the everyday moments of our lives. By cultivating a sense of mindfulness, gratitude, and compassion, we can tap into this transcendent power of love and create relationships that are truly transformative. So, take the time to appreciate the wonder and

The Alchemy of Affection

mystery of love, and let it guide you on a journey of spiritual growth and connection.

♥♥

CONCLUSION: THE ALCHEMICAL JOURNEY OF LOVE

As you conclude your transformative journey, remember this wisdom: do not take love too seriously. Good times and challenging moments come and go like the tides of life. By carrying a smile and a lighthearted attitude, you will navigate the path with greater ease, inviting love to find its way to you.

When you approach love with a willingness to play, and a contagious good attitude, you will radiate an irresistible magnetism that draws love closer.

Embrace a childlike wonder, playfulness, and creativity to complement all you've discovered in *The Alchemy of Affection*. After each "Alchemy" exercise, consider incorporating moments of lightheartedness through engaging in playful activities together. This might involve playing board games, taking dance classes, visiting a playground, enjoying a swing ride, or playing in the sand. Choose any activity or hobby that brings you both joy. Doing so will reinforce the positive emotions associated with enhancing your relationship.

Ways In Which Incorporating Play And Creativity Can Be Beneficial

Bonding and Connection: Engaging in playful activities strengthens the bond between you and your partner. Sharing laughter and fun creates positive memories and fosters a sense of shared enjoyment, which can deepen your emotional intimacy.

Stress Relief: Playfulness provides an opportunity to escape daily stresses and challenges. Lighthearted activities let you let go of worries and experience a sense of freedom, relaxation, and rejuvenation.

Communication and Understanding: Playfulness encourages open communication and facilitates understanding. When engaging in playful interactions, both partners tend to let down their guards, leading to increased vulnerability and the ability to express thoughts, feelings, and desires in a non-threatening manner.

Creativity and Exploration: Playfulness stimulates creativity and encourages exploration within the relationship. Engaging in imaginative activities can spark new ideas, inspire spontaneity, and bring novelty into your partnership, preventing stagnation and boredom.

Physical Intimacy: Playfulness can also enhance physical intimacy in a relationship. Engaging in playful touch, flirtation, or exploring new experiences can reignite passion, deepen trust, and bring you closer.

Longevity and Relationship Satisfaction: Couples with a playful attitude tend to have more satisfying and enduring relationships. Playfulness helps you navigate challenges with resilience, keeps the relationship dynamic, and promotes a positive outlook on life together.

Having joyful fun together may come naturally after a while, but at first, set aside time for trying new hobbies, engaging in playful banter, or simply having a time for laughter and playfulness.

Example

Here is an example of how a couple incorporated a sense of wonder and play into their relationship:

Linda and James

Linda and James created a playful adventure by exploring a new hobby together - painting. They set up a small art corner in their home with easels, paintbrushes, and various vibrant paints.

They designated a few hours every weekend as their "art playtime." They let their imaginations run wild during these sessions, experimenting with colors, textures, and painting techniques. It is not about creating masterpieces; instead, they focus on the joy of self-expression and being together.

As they paint, laughter fills the room, and they reminisce about their childhood. They take breaks to admire each other's work, playfully teasing and exchanging compliments.

Through their playful painting adventures, Linda and James find joy in the process, reminding them to embrace the simple pleasures and approach life with a childlike spirit. They carry this playfulness beyond their art sessions, finding increased joy in everyday moments and cultivating a love that continues to flourish over the long term.

Conclusion

As you embrace this alchemical journey of love, remember that it is a process that requires patience, dedication, and commitment with an added spark of fun. Love is ultimately a gift. It is a gift we give ourselves and others, bringing joy, meaning, and fulfillment to our lives. It is a gift that can transform us, heal us, and help us reach our full potential as human beings.

So, as you continue your journey of love, remember to savor the moments of joy and connection, to be grateful for the blessings in your life, and to approach the challenges with a childlike spirit of curiosity and growth.

HOPE FOR LOVE

It's important to remember that no relationship is perfect, despite what some people may portray. Every couple faces challenges, and through these struggles, we learn, grow, and ultimately become stronger. Embrace the difficulties and give yourself credit for wanting to evolve. By reading this book, you are already taking a step in the right direction and demonstrating a commitment to personal growth. Remember that struggles are an essential part of the journey and can lead to a more fulfilling relationship in the long run.

Don't give up on love. Having trouble and difficult times does not mean all hope is lost. Do not give up on having amazing love in your life. Where you are in life right now is precisely where you need to be, and struggles are just a part of the process. If you are not yet in a relationship, keep learning, growing, and placing your soul in a ready and open place for the love you deserve (The topic for my next book). Life and love can change in an instant. Your very next step could be the one that opens the door to a deep, profound, and everlasting love.

From Dr. Kevin Grold:

I hope The Alchemy of Affection has been a valuable resource in your journey toward a fulfilling and loving relationship. I also hope that its insights and guidance inspire and enrich your connection with your partner and that your relationship is a source of joy, kindness, and beauty radiating out into the world.

♥♥

ABOUT THE AUTHOR

Dr. Kevin Grold has a Ph.D. in clinical psychology. His first book, *The Love Report,* is based on his research into couples in long-term relationships. He has always had an interest in the topic of love and making it easy for others to understand and integrate love into their life. He has been sought out for advice from Dear Abby more than a few times and he has created many self-help tests used around the world. For over a decade, he ran the international therapist referral service 1-800-therapist.com and then for the next twenty years, he was the CEO of EDReferral.com, which is the largest online referral service for eating disorders. He is currently a volunteer CASA Court Appointed Special Advocate for foster youth, and he lives in Del Mar, California, with his dog, Happy.

Dr. Kevin Grold

Photo credit here and on the cover: Mariola Hupert

Continue the discussion and learning here:

www.thealchemyoflove.com

The Love Report can be found here:

www.tinyurl.com/kevingrold

The Alchemy of Affection

From Dr. Grold's first book, *The Love Report*:

Definition of love: Love is an emotional, sexual, and security-creating experience between two people that grows over time and results from committing to the process of sharing yourself, understanding your partner, and actively participating in making the relationship better.

https://tinyurl.com/TheLoveReport

Dr. Kevin Grold

Thank you for purchasing and reading The Alchemy of Affection. I hope you found value in reading it. Please consider leaving a review online. Your feedback allows me to reach more people and help others who need wigs while dealing with cancer. Please go to https://tinyurl.com/AlchemyRev if you would like to leave a review.

The Alchemy of Affection

Dr. Kevin Grold

www.ingramcontent.com/pod-product-compliance
Lightning Source LLC
Chambersburg PA
CBHW051544010526
44118CB00022B/2570